HERBIE KNOTT

AN INDEPENDENT EYE

THE HULTON GETTY
PICTURE COLLECTION
& THE INDEPENDENT

F. J. MORTIMER

An Independent Eye

A Century of Photographs

Roger Hudson

SUTTON PUBLISHING

PETER JAY

(Half-title picture)
A transvestite (Petit Chou) at the wheel of a 1928 Ford AA flatbed cabbage lorry in Spitalfields Market, London, taking part in Alternative Fashion Week in March 1994.

(Title page picture)
Strawberry pickers in a Hampshire field at the turn of the century pause for a break and a youthful smoke.

Venus Williams
the American tennis player happy after a practice session at Roehampton Club in June 1998 (left), *shortly before the Wimbledon Championships.*

First published in 1998 by
Sutton Publishing · Phoenix Mill
Thrupp · Stroud · Gloucestershire · GL5 2BU

Copyright © The Hulton Getty Picture Collection 1998

British Library Cataloguing in Publication Data
A catalogue record for this book is available from the British Library

ISBN 0-7509-2107-2 (case)
ISBN 0-7509-2127-7 (paper)

Project manager: Richard Collins
Designer: Paul Welti
Picture researcher: Alex Linghorn
Scanner: Antonia Hille
Typesetter: Peter Howard

Typeset in Frutiger
Origination by Jade Reprographics Ltd
Printed in Great Britain by Butler & Tanner, Frome, Somerset

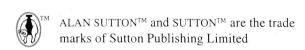

An Independent Eye is the result of the work of many different parties. It was inspired by Photo 98, the UK Year of Photography and the Electronic Image. Anne McNeill of Photo 98 and David Swanborough at the *Independent*, working with David Allison at The Hulton Getty Picture Collection, sifted through thousands of images to select an individual photograph for each year of the century. This quirky selection was featured daily for three months in the *Independent* newspaper where it quickly acquired a dedicated following.

Photo 98 was created as part of an Arts Council initiative to celebrate a different art form for each year through to the millennium. Its aim has been to raise the profile of creative photography in the UK. The image on this page of a woman from Chechnya was selected for "10 x 8", one of the first major exhibitions commissioned by Photo 98.

This book is a further development of the day by day concept. The images chosen reflect the vast resources of The Hulton Getty Picture Collection which dates back to the very beginning of photography in the middle of the nineteenth century and now incorporates well over 12 million images. These include some of the world's greatest photojournalism, ranging from pictures by *Picture Post* news photographers Bert Hardy and Thurston Hopkins to Keystone Press photographers Fred Ramage and Ron Case and many more, as can be seen in the following pages.

Of all the daily newspapers published in the British Isles today, the *Independent* is the most committed to the very best of contemporary

During the Chechnya offensive
in August 1996 a woman emerges from an air raid shelter to the horror and destruction of the central market in Grozny (below).

STANLEY GREENE

photography. Continuing the great tradition of photojournalism, the paper has contributed images from its own archives and these are represented in the many extraordinary and striking images for the years 1986 (when the *Independent* was launched) to 1999.

Sutton Publishing is one of the most successful publishers of history in the country, with an expansive list and an approach that is both academic and popular. *An Independent Eye* therefore represents a meeting of like minds – The Hulton Getty Picture Collection, the *Independent*, Photo 98 and Sutton Publishing – all united in a firm commitment to history, photography and photojournalism.

Looming over harbour traffic,
the pirate galleon Neptune *dominates the Marseille waterfront. Built especially for Roman Polanski's film,* Pirates, *and photographed in 1992, it remains in its berth to this day.*

7

1900

In January Lord Roberts becomes Commander-in-Chief of the British Army fighting the Boers in South Africa, with Kitchener as his chief of staff. After a string of defeats, Britain's fortunes begin to take a turn for the better under this new leadership. The besieged town of Ladysmith is relieved in February and then Colonel Baden-Powell, later to found the Boy Scouts, is relieved at Mafeking in May, which causes wild rejoicing in England. By the end of the year both the Orange Free State and the Transvaal have been annexed by Britain, but the Boers are stepping up their guerrilla warfare. The Boxer Rebellion breaks out in China in June and the European legations in Peking are besieged until an international relief force arrives in August. Arthur Evans' excavations at Knossos in Crete begin to uncover the remains of the Minoan civilisation from the second millennium BC. Speech is transmitted for the first time by the wireless. The first motor bus runs in Britain and the first international motor car race is held in France. The Paris Metro opens. The Brownie box camera is introduced by Eastman Kodak in the USA. Sigmund Freud's *The Interpretation of Dreams* and Joseph Conrad's *Lord Jim* are published. Puccini's *Tosca*, Mahler's Fourth Symphony, Elgar's *Dream of Gerontius*, G. B. Shaw's *You Never Can Tell* and Anton Chekhov's *Uncle Vanya* have their first performances.

Off to the Exhibition.
Smart Parisians are pushed to the Exposition Internationale of 1900 down one of the wide new boulevards of the French capital. The bath chairs in which they ride have been adapted, with the steering tillers to the front wheels removed and mudguards added to preserve the elegant dresses of the ladies. Anyone whose feet have suffered at a modern trade fair must envy this mode of transport. By the end of the 19th century international exhibitions have become a regular feature of life in Europe and North America, expressions of national pride and rivalries, shop windows for industry and commerce. The Eiffel Tower had been erected for the 1889 Exhibition in Paris. The Grand and Petit Palais have been built for this one. The gold medals awarded at exhibitions still linger on the labels of old-established products.

1901

Queen Victoria dies on 22 January and is succeeded by her son, Edward VII. During the course of the year, negotiations for an Anglo-German alliance gradually break down. President McKinley of the United States is shot by a Polish-American anarchist and on his death in September Theodore (Teddy) Roosevelt becomes President. Marconi transmits wireless messages from Cornwall to Newfoundland and Britain sees its first motor bike. *Kim* by Rudyard Kipling and *Buddenbrooks* by Thomas Mann are published. Rachmaninov's Second Piano Concerto, Chekhov's *Three Sisters* and Strindberg's *Dance of Death* have their first performances.

F. J. MORTIMER

A Boer markswoman,

*Mrs Otto Krantz (opposite), poses for the camera in smart riding habit
and jaunty slouch hat towards the conclusion of the Boer War (1899–1902).
There are few concessions to the practicalities of war in her dress or her equipment – that is
a side-saddle on the horse. She took part in the early Boer defeat at Elandslaagte in October 1899
and in the fighting on the Tugela River in January 1900. By 1901 such set-pieces are long over and
the Boers are fighting a guerrilla war, while their families are rounded up into concentration camps
so they cannot supply their men. Disease and malnutrition in the camps are the biggest killers of
all – 26,000 women and children die. Women's clothes in Britain are no more practical,
whether one is a lady in mittens pouring tea (above right), a maid trying her
hand at croquet (above left), or balancing extravagant headgear like
these chorus girls from the show* The Matinee Hat *(top left).*

1902

Britain ends its isolation by signing an agreement with Japan to maintain the independence of China and Korea. The Boer War ends in May. Nearly 6,000 British have been killed and 16,000 have died of disease. Arthur Balfour succeeds his uncle Lord Salisbury as Conservative Prime Minister in July. The Education Act provides for secondary schools. Cuba gains its independence from Spain. Ibn Saud seizes Riyadh, so marking the beginnings of Saudi Arabia. The artificial fibre rayon is patented in the USA. *The Hound of the Baskervilles* by Arthur Conan Doyle, *Peter Rabbit* by Beatrix Potter, and *Just So Stories* by Rudyard Kipling are published. The opera *Pélleas et Mélisande* by Debussy is performed for the first time.

BENJAMIN STONE

Pomp and circumstance.

The Coronation coach conveys King Edward VII and Queen Alexandra to Westminster Abbey (left). Originally planned for 26 June, the ceremony has to be post-poned until 9 August when the King gets appendicitis. Edward Elgar composed the music for a Coronation Ode, not performed until November, which includes his 'Land of Hope and Glory' and in turn becomes part of his 'Pomp and Circumstance' marches. During the ceremony, the King has to help the aged and infirm Archbishop of Canterbury to his feet when he is unable to rise from the kneeling position. Participants include representatives of the Indian Army (top left) and choristers of the Chapel Royal (top right). As shown by these views of the Empire Music Hall in Leicester Square and Queen Victoria Street (above left and right), the capital is fully decorated for the occasion.

1903

The British conquest of northern Nigeria is completed. Edward VII's visit to Paris in May and the visit of the French Premier to London in July signal the beginning of the Entente Cordiale alliance between the two countries. Joseph Chamberlain resigns from the British Government so that he can champion the cause of Imperial Preference, which seeks to penalise imports not from the British Empire. Russia looks to expand its empire into Manchuria and Korea. The Russian Social Democrats split at their London Congress and the Bolshevik Party emerges, led by Lenin and Trotsky. Mrs Pankhurst founds the Women's Social and Political Union which becomes the centrepiece of the suffragettes' movement seeking votes for women. The Wright brothers make their successful flight in a petrol-engined aeroplane in the United States. London sees its first motor taxis. Henry James publishes *The Ambassadors* and G. B. Shaw's play *Man and Superman* has its first night.

REINHOLD THIELE

A dancing bear

in an outer London street stops the children on their way to school (left). Its handler has not had to blow his bugle to attract this audience, but they are unlikely to give him much for his pains. The gramophone and the cinema may just be making their presence felt, but street entertainers – Italian organ grinders with their performing monkeys, German bands – can still scrape a living in these early decades of the electronic age. The first electric tram goes into service in 1903, but roads are still lit by gas lamps, like the one on the left. The boys' knickerbockers reflect the ideas of the dress reformers prevalent since the 1880s. To see these freaks of human nature (above) you would have to pay good money at Barnum's Menagerie. From the left: Laloo (two bodies), Young Herman (expanding chest), J. K. Coffey (skeleton body), James Morris (elasticated skin) and Jo Jo (the dog-faced man).

PAUL MARTIN

BOYER D'AGEN

Carmelite nuns
*at prayer, while one of their number prostrates herself in worship,
in the shape of the cross, before the altar* (right). *Another kneels before a
devotional picture of Jesus* (above), *with her arms outstretched, in her cell. A skull
below the crucifix at the head of her bed is there as a* memento mori. *The
kettle at the foot is, however, a reassuring touch.*

BOYER D'AGEN

1904

In February Japanese torpedo boats launch a surprise attack on the Russian fleet anchored at Port Arthur in north China, starting the Russo-Japanese War and foreshadowing Japan's surprise attack on the US Pacific fleet at Pearl Harbor in 1941. In April the Entente Cordiale is formally enshrined in an Anglo-French treaty. In November the first submarine journey takes place, from Portsmouth to the Isle of Wight, while *Peter Pan* by J. M. Barrie has its first performance on Boxing Day. At the beginning of the year *The Cherry Orchard* by Anton Chekhov had opened in Moscow and *Madam Butterfly* by Puccini in Milan.

REINHOLD THIELE

1905

Although not an outright Japanese victory, the Battle of Mukden in March ends with 70,000 Russians killed. When Russia's Baltic fleet finally arrives in the Far East in May, it is shot out of the water by the Japanese. A peace is signed in September. This humiliating defeat leads to demonstrations, strikes and massacres within Russia itself, culminating in the promise of an elective assembly from the new Tsar, Nicholas II. It also demonstrates to fledgling nationalist movements all over Asia that European powers are not invincible. Another certainty to crumble is the idea of Time and Mass both being fixed, succumbing to Albert Einstein's Theory of Relativity published in September. A new absolute is erected in their stead, the speed of light, than which nothing can go faster. In response to public demand, Arthur Conan Doyle resurrects his most popular creation in *The Return of Sherlock Holmes*. Norway gains its independence from Sweden.

F. BEZANCON

A Royal Navy recruiting office,

where a youth is inspected by a Petty Officer (opposite) *to see whether he has the makings to become
an Able Bodied Seaman, the lowest rank in the service. In the 1890s the Navy had undergone a great expansion
and this continued in the 1900s, as Germany started to build its own battlefleet. The first of Britain's dreadnoughts,
'all-big-gun' battleships, is laid down in October 1905. In the Russian fleet, defeat by the Japanese brings mutiny in
its wake, aboard the battleship* Potemkin *at Odessa in the Black Sea. The mutineers come ashore to give
themselves up in the nearby Romanian port of Constanta* (above). *Their mutiny will be immortalised in
1925 by the great Russian film maker, Sergei Eisenstein, in* The Battleship Potemkin.

1906

The Liberal Party wins a landslide victory in the British General Election in February, though twenty-nine Labour MPs are also elected. Social reform is very much on the agenda and, if the new suffragettes have their way, so too will be votes for women. San Francisco is devastated by an earthquake and still more damage is done by subsequent fires, leaving 250,000 homeless. Permanent waves for women are introduced in London, cornflakes are invented by William Kellogg, and the electric washing-machine appears for the first time. John Galsworthy publishes the first volume of *The Forsyte Saga*. HMS *Dreadnought*, the first modern battleship, is launched in February, rendering every other battleship obsolete and initiating a naval armaments race in Europe, Japan and the USA.

Belfast children
playing in the street (above) look well cared for and dressed, though some have no shoes.

A class at an infants' school
in Chelsea (left). The strain of holding the pose for the camera has been too much for one child in the front row. Primary education for all only became compulsory in 1870. Both before and after that date many schools were run by the different churches, like this Roman Catholic one belonging to the Chelsea Oratory. There is no trace of child-centred learning here, as the children face the blackboard, out of shot. The mistress has moved from her normal position, in front of the whole class, so as to be included in the photograph.

1907

The Liberal Government at Westminster runs up against a campaign in the House of Lords to wreck its legislative programme, so determines to introduce a bill to curb the Lords' power of veto. Robert Baden-Powell, the hero of Mafeking, launches the Boy Scout Movement. Cubism, one of the great innovations of modern art, is launched with Picasso's painting of a group of Barcelona prostitutes, *Les Demoiselles d'Avignon*. Reacting against Romanticism and Impressionism, the strongest influence detectable in this particular work is primitive African sculpture. Richard Strauss's opera *Salomé* opens in New York and is soon banned, while the first night of J. M. Synge's *The Playboy of the Western World* causes a riot in Dublin when Nationalists see in it a slight offered to Irish womanhood. The artistic situation is perhaps redeemed when Kipling becomes the first British writer to win the Nobel Prize. In medicine, chemotherapy and blood transfusions are introduced.

London flower 'girls'

with their baskets on a traffic island (left). Here they avoid prosecution by the police for obstructing the pavement. They will have bought their stock very early in the morning at Covent Garden wholesale market before carrying it to their regular pitch. The most famous is round the statue of Eros at Piccadilly Circus. A few years later, George Bernard Shaw will make a flower girl, Eliza Doolittle, the heroine of his play Pygmalion. *They have to put up with extremes of weather and exhaust fumes from motor buses, taxis and cars. A trap drawn by a tame zebra, however, is no hazard to health (top). Why does it take two City policemen (above) to help the old lady across Threadneedle Street?*

1908

Herbert Asquith becomes Liberal Prime Minister with David Lloyd George as his Chancellor of the Exchequer. Old Age Pensions are announced – five shillings a week from the age of seventy. Germany launches its first dreadnought-type battleship. Pu Yi, China's last emperor, comes to the throne. In the Balkans, Bosnia and Herzegovina are absorbed into the Austro-Hungarian Empire, while Bulgaria becomes independent of the Turkish Empire. A meteorite hits Siberia in June, causing the world's largest ever explosion, and 80,000 are killed at Messina in Sicily by an earthquake on 28 December. The first Model T Ford motor car is produced, to be followed by 16½ million more. *The Wind in the Willows* by Kenneth Grahame and *A Room with a View* by E. M. Forster are published.

The Franco-British Exhibition

at the White City, west London (right), *is held to celebrate the four-year-old Entente Cordiale between the two countries. Forty acres of gleaming white buildings, floodlit at night with the new electric light, include as their centrepiece the Hall of Honour, with its surrounding Indian pavilions reflected in the lake. (India is regarded as the 'jewel in the crown' of Britain's empire.) The Entente may have been the final gesture to signal the end of France's role as Britain's traditional enemy, but it also served to increase Germany's fears of encirclement by the newly emergent alliance of Britain, France and Russia. There is also a sports stadium built at White City where the Olympic Games are held later that summer. High drama attends the finish of the Marathon when the Italian Dorando Pietri staggers just before the finish, is then supported across the line, and so disqualified from winning* (above).

REINHOLD THIELE

1909

Lloyd George introduces his People's Budget, largely to pay for six more dreadnought battleships: death duties to be increased, a 'supertax' on incomes above £3,000 and a tax on land values. The House of Lords flings the budget out. The Liberals win the election that follows, but with a reduced majority. The suffragettes' campaign continues, with 120 being arrested outside the Houses of Parliament. Some are forcibly fed while in prison. In Paris Sergei Diaghilev's Ballets Russes, starring Nijinsky and Anna Pavlova, transfixes the artistic world. In the USA, prohibition of alcohol is spreading rapidly state by state. The American Commander Perry reaches the North Pole. Thirty thousand Armenians are massacred in Turkey.

The French aviator

Louis Blériot becomes the first man to fly across the English Channel on 25 July, crash-landing after a 43 minute flight on the hills behind Dover. The next day he and his wife pose by his frail monoplane (left), held together with piano wire and weighing only 45 pounds. He had no compass and found his way over the sea by following the ships below, until he saw a journalist waving a French tricolour flag to indicate where he could land. Blériot is piloting a later model (above), the Blériot XII, its wings above his head rather than below him. He constantly modifies his designs and has already tried biplanes and a tail-first monoplane.

1910

King Edward VII dies in May and his successor, George V, is confronted almost immediately with a constitutional crisis caused by Asquith's determination to end the Lords' veto of legislation. The new King agrees to make enough Liberal peers to outnumber the Tories, provided Asquith wins yet one more election. He does, and the threat of a Liberal influx is enough to secure the compliance of the Lords. All this takes place against a background of industrial unrest, with railwaymen, miners and shipbuilders on strike at various times. The first film is made in Hollywood and the tango becomes a craze on the dance floor. Wassily Kandinsky adds Abstraction to Cubism in the repertoire of modern art.

An overfurnished salon

lined with the small antlers of chamois mountain deer in Schloss Konopischt (right), a Bohemian castle belonging to Archduke Franz Ferdinand. He is heir to Franz Joseph, ruler of the Austro-Hungarian Empire, of which Bohemia (in the present-day Czech Republic) is part, and married to a Czech countess, so it is very natural for him to have a home here. By the standards of the hide-bound Imperial Court at Vienna he is of a liberal and reforming tendency with sympathy for the Empire's Slav minorities, from which his wife comes. This does not prevent their assassination in June 1914 at Sarajevo, the capital of Bosnia, by south Slav nationalists from Serbia – the event which sets in train the outbreak of World War One. Another keen princely shot, the Russian Grand Duke Michael Mikhailovich, accompanied by his daughter, the Countess Zia Torby, waits for the pheasants at the Earl of Craven's shoot at Coombe Abbey (above).

1911

Germany increases its army by half a million men. The rule of the Manchu emperors in China comes to an end when revolution breaks out, organised by the Kuomintang Party led by Sun Yat-sen. It promotes the idea of democratic government and social reform. In Russia the ruthless but reforming Prime Minister Peter Stolypin is assassinated – with him dies the last best hope of the country avoiding violent upheaval. The Norwegian explorer Roald Amundsen reaches the South Pole ahead of the British team led by Captain Scott. He and four companions perish on the return journey from the Pole.

A peeress
*outside Westminster Abbey
at the conclusion of the Coronation
of King George V. She is escorted by a
Grenadier Guards officer, one of the fifty
gentlemen summoned as 'Gold Staff Officers'
by the Earl Marshal, organiser of the Coronation,
to usher guests to their places in the Abbey.
His gold staff is under his arm and he smokes a
no doubt long-anticipated cigarette. It is either
Turkish or Egyptian – Guards officers do not
smoke Virginia cigarettes. At the time of Edward
VII's Coronation the peeresses petitioned
the King for permission to wear their tiaras
as well as their coronets, as
this lady does here.*

1912

A Bill to give Home Rule to Ireland meets bitter opposition from the northern, largely Protestant, counties of Ulster and is rejected by the House of Lords. The *Titanic* liner, built in a Belfast shipyard, sinks on its maiden voyage across the Atlantic in April. Serbia, Bulgaria, Greece and Montenegro form the Balkan League and wrest nearly all Turkey's remaining lands in Europe from her. The new state of Albania emerges. Woodrow Wilson is elected US President and a bomb explodes inside the ceremonial elephant-borne howdah of the Viceroy, Lord Hardinge, in India, badly wounding him. The first crossword, neon lights, and self service food store are seen.

Two small boys,
who look suspiciously like twins,
are suspended in harnesses by ropes fixed to boat
hooks, in the Thames at Wallingford (left). Judging by the
number of spectators on the bank and afloat, this may
well be an event at the local regatta, a swimming race for
non-swimmers perhaps. 'Messing about on the river' was one of
the many sports which became crazes from the 1880s on, like
tennis and golf, helping to fill the leisure hours of the well-off
who are able to pursue them thanks to the greater mobility
afforded by the railways, motor cars and bicycles. If you can't
afford the real thing, you can still race model boats, like these
enthusiasts at Victoria Park in east London (above).

1913

A Bill to give women the vote is defeated in the House of Commons. Emily Davison becomes a suffragette martyr by trying to seize the reins of, and falling under the hooves of, King George V's horse in this year's Derby. She dies four days later. The Irish Home Rule Bill is again rejected by the House of Lords. The former members of the Balkan League fight among themselves, Bulgaria being attacked by Greece, Serbia, Romania and Turkey. Mahatma Gandhi is jailed in India for leading a passive resistance movement to British rule. The first volume of Marcel Proust's *A la recherche du temps perdu* is published and D. H. Lawrence's *Sons and Lovers*.

The Flat Iron Building
in New York (above), a twenty-storey skyscraper on a triangular site, was completed in 1902. This limestone wedge, where Broadway meets Fifth Avenue, has become a city landmark.

Going up.
A construction team working on one of the new skyscraper buildings in the United States put on the nonchalance for the photographer as they hitch a ride on a crane (opposite). Until the introduction of steel framing in the 1880s there was a limit to how high buildings could go – not much more than 300 feet. By 1914 the Woolworth Building in New York had reached just under 800 feet. The Empire State Building (1932) was 1,250 feet. The other necessary ingredient of the skyscraper was the high-speed elevator.

1914

Fifty-eight cavalry officers stationed outside Dublin say they would prefer dismissal rather than having to coerce Ulster into complying with Irish Home Rule legislation. They are not relieved of their posts. Both nationalists in the south and loyalists in the north of Ireland are receiving arms shipments. Civil war looms as the Home Rule Bill enters its final phase, but world war breaks out first, sparked by the assassination of Archduke Franz Ferdinand of Austria on 28 June (see 1910, p.28). When Austria declares war on Serbia on 28 July it prompts Russian mobilisation. Germany declares war on Russia, which brings about French mobilisation. Finally, Britain commits herself once German troops advance onto Belgian soil. The German aim, to knock out France quickly before turning her full forces on Russia, is foiled by the French counter-offensive on the Marne. The war is going to be a long one and soon movement is replaced by a stalemate as the trenches of the Western Front are dug. *Tarzan of the Apes* by Edgar Rice Burroughs is published, and the zip and the brassiere are invented. The first ship sails through the Panama Canal.

An American suffragette

addresses her audience, which has been attracted by the beating of a drum (opposite). In England a favourite suffragette tactic is to protest outside Buckingham Palace (above right), and the women often try to chain themselves to its railings. In the War they are to march under banners demanding the right to work, which is given in full measure. Male preserves, such as London's transport system, are infiltrated by girls like this snow-covered bus conductress (above left).

1915

In April the Germans are the first to use gas, at Ypres, and the Allies land troops at Gallipoli in an attempt to force the Dardanelles narrows and take Germany's ally, Turkey, in the rear. But the Turks are ready and the Allies gain little more than a foothold, at the cost of many lives. Attacks at Neuve Chapelle and Loos on the Western Front are equally costly, so it is as well that 3 million volunteers flock to join Kitchener battalions at home. The first of them are wasted in further futile attacks at Gallipoli in August. Lloyd George becomes Minister for Munitions and General Haig is made Commander-in-Chief in France. The torpedoing of the liner *Lusitania* with Americans on board in May will eventually help to bring the USA into the war against Germany. The Turks slaughter up to 1½ million Armenians. In October Nurse Edith Cavell is shot by the Germans in Brussels for helping Allied prisoners escape to neutral Holland. Allied troops are evacuated from Gallipoli at the end of the year.

A troupe of pierrots and pierrettes
*pose for a publicity shot on the open top of
a bus in the West End of London. The Russell Street
colonnade (1831) of the Drury Lane Theatre is behind.
Its cast-iron columns used to be painted red, earning it
the nickname of Rhubarb Alley. Pierrot troupes, betraying
their very distant Commedia dell'Arte ancestry in their
baggy white costumes, are particularly associated
with seaside entertainment, where their simple songs
and patter keep holidaymakers happy. London looked
for something more sophisticated, like the revue at
the Alhambra Music Hall in Leicester Square being
advertised on the front of the bus, but in wartime
the civilian population and troops home on
leave would settle for any distraction.*

1916

The Germans launch an attack on the French fortress at Verdun in February and huge casualties begin to mount on both sides. A small group of Nationalists launch the Easter Rising in Dublin. They are easily defeated, but the execution of fifteen of them gives their cause the martyrs it needs. On 1 June the fleets of Britain and Germany meet at Jutland. The battle is inconclusive, but the German fleet never ventures out again. On 1 July General Haig starts the battle of the Somme. By the time it ends, five miles have been gained for 620,000 Allied dead, and tanks have had their baptism of fire. It does, however, relieve German pressure on the French at Verdun. They have lost 400,000 there, the Germans 350,000. In Mesopotamia an Anglo-Indian army surrenders to the Turks at Kut in April. Romania and Italy join the Allies. In the USA, the Coca-Cola bottle is introduced and James Joyce's *A Portrait of the Artist as a Young Man* is published.

Vermin control.

German soldiers with their bag of rats after a hunt through their living quarters (above). *Their trenches and dug-outs were generally much more solidly built and deeper than the Allies', like the one in the background, but that did not stop the arrival of the rodents.*

A German army dog,

used to detect mines and tunnels being dug, find soldiers buried by shell bursts, or carry messages. It has been made a fool of by a French photographer dressing it in a German soldier's cap and glasses, and equipping it with binoculars (opposite). *Some years after the end of the War, an ex-German army dog called Rin Tin Tin will become a huge movie star.*

1917

The strain of war on the Russian social fabric is too much, and in February a revolution begins. Tsar Nicholas II abdicates in March, but the provisional Republican Government that replaces him goes on fighting Germany. The German U-boat campaign sinks more than a million tons of shipping in April, but the USA enters the war in the same month, which is as well since fifty-four of the one hundred French divisions refuse orders until Marshal Pétain promises that they will not have to take part in any more major offensives. Lloyd George by now is Prime Minister but is unable to prevent Haig's 'summer' offensive at Passchendaele, which grinds to a halt in deep mud in November. T. E. Lawrence and General Allenby achieve success against the Turks in Arabia and Palestine but the Italian front collapses against the Austrians. The Bolsheviks stage a coup in St Petersburg in October, and start to construct 'the Socialist order'. Peace talks between the new Communist Russia and Germany start in December.

A star shell

*or flare lends a deceptive gaiety to the
night sky on the Western Front in Flanders,
outlining a tin-hatted Tommy and the posts supporting
a barbed-wire entanglement. The previous year was
bad enough, with the Somme and Verdun,
but this year is no better.*

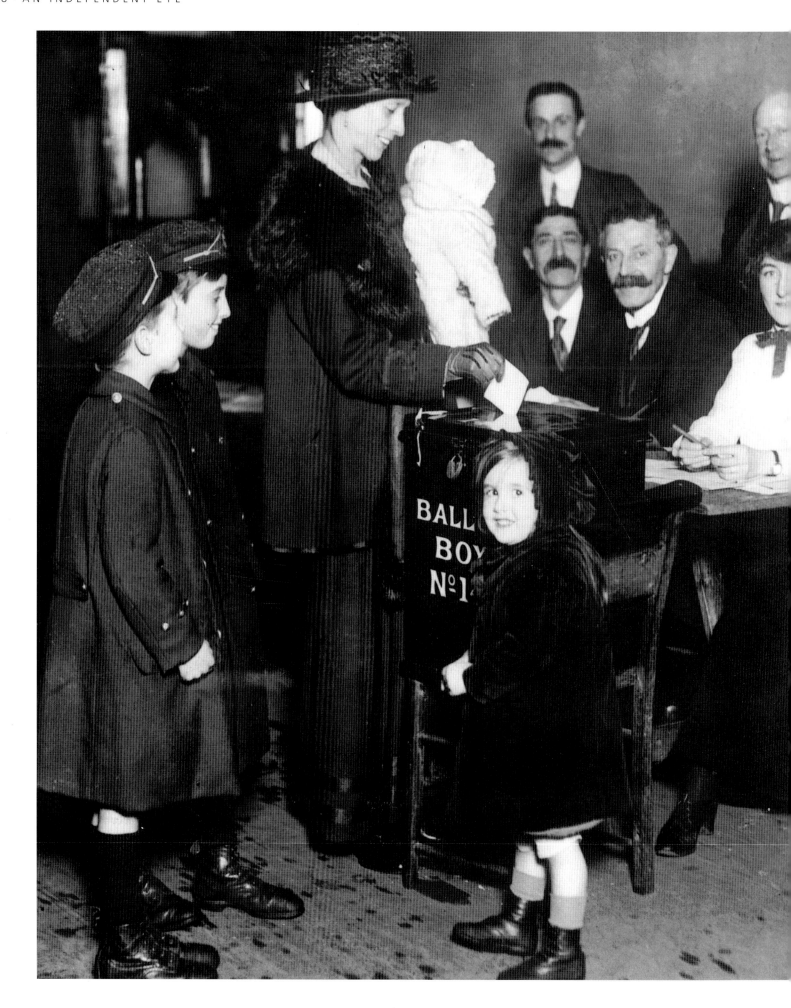

A.R. COSTER

1918

The Germans, desperate for a knock-out blow before the new American divisions flood into France, and able to switch troops from the Eastern to the Western Front because of Russia's withdrawal from the war, launch a great offensive in March. British forces reel back forty miles. There is a further big push in April, but it peters out by the end of the month. The last German offensive comes in July, but Marshal Foch, Supreme Allied Commander, counter-attacks vigorously and the Franco-American-British forces are soon advancing on all fronts, with tanks and planes playing an important part. The Armistice comes on 11 November. In Russia counter-revolutionary 'White' forces are fighting a bitter civil war with the 'Red' Communists. The Russian Royal Family are shot by the Reds for fear that they might be rescued by the Whites. The Russian, Austro-Hungarian, Turkish, and German Empires are no more.

A woman votes

for the first time in a British General Election (left), *six weeks after the end of the War. She qualifies to do so because she is over thirty. It is feared that, without this condition, the women will outnumber the men. In fact, there turn out to be over 13 million men and 8^1/$_2$ million women eligible to vote in 1919. It is not a straightforward party fight because the wartime coalition is guaranteed to continue by the arrangement that 150 Liberal candidates can stand unopposed by the Conservatives. What people want is for Lloyd George, the man who won the War, to continue in power and fulfil his promise to make Britain 'a fit country for heroes to live in'. In the autumn the great influenza epidemic hits Britain and precautions include masks as well as disinfectant spraying of buses* (above).

1919

British troops are fighting the Reds in Russia, and the Royal Irish Constabulary are under attack from the Irish Republican Army. Nancy Astor is the first woman MP to take her seat at Westminster. In Germany the Spartacists (Communists) stage an unsuccessful revolt and their leaders, Rosa Luxemburg and Karl Liebknecht, are murdered. The punitive terms imposed on Germany by the Treaty of Versailles, signed in June, play into the hands of such right-wing parties as the National Socialists, soon being addressed by an ex-corporal of the Bavarian army, Adolf Hitler. Rutherford splits the atom for the first time, while Alcock and Brown fly the Atlantic non-stop. The influenza epidemic kills more people world-wide – possibly up to 20 million – than were killed in the War.

German Communists
demonstrate under their new symbol of the hammer and sickle and the red star outside a building redolent of the old order they seek to sweep away (above).

Allied officers
stand on tables and chairs, determined not to miss the historic moment when the Treaty of Versailles, settling the terms to be imposed on Germany (left), is signed in the Galerie des Glaces, the Hall of Mirrors there. It had witnessed the creation of the German Empire in 1871 after the defeat of France in the Franco-Prussian War.

1920

The Royal Irish Constabulary are reinforced by new recruits from Britain, the Black and Tans, and later by ex-officer Auxiliaries. British regular forces are also involved in the increasingly bitter guerrilla war with the IRA. A new Home Rule Bill outlines separate parliaments for Ulster and for the south. The Reds gradually get the upper hand over the Whites in Russia, but their attack on newly independent Poland is repulsed. The manufacture and sale of alcohol is banned in the USA, ushering in the golden age of the gangsters, rum runners, bootleggers and speakeasies. The gangsters' favourite weapon, the tommy gun, is invented, as is the Bloody Mary cocktail.

A pig shed

*is home for this family in Woking, Surrey (above),
struggling to maintain standards of cleanliness and
respectability against the odds.*

Derby Day

*at Epsom and King George V has come to
enjoy the racing – the Sport of Kings. He travels in an
open carriage (right), continuing pre-war customs and
ignoring the comfort offered by the motor car. But reality
breaks in, in the form of a beggar keeping pace with the
trotting horses. The most remarkable feature of
the picture is the complete absence of
uniformed police or security men
to protect the King.*

1921

Britain's post-war boom comes to an end with 2 million out of work, the miners unsuccessfully on strike and agricultural wages halved. A truce is agreed with Sinn Fein, the Irish Nationalists, in June. Mustafa Kemal, later Kemal Atatürk, becomes ruler of Turkey and starts to push back the invading Greeks. Mussolini and his Fascists win thirty-five seats in the Italian parliament. Hitler becomes leader of the National Socialist Workers' Party in Germany, where the currency begins to collapse in November. A way to manufacture insulin for the treatment of diabetes is invented, Chanel No. 5 perfume goes on sale and Marie Stopes opens her first birth control clinic.

Famine comes to Russia

on the heels of the civil war between Reds and Whites (opposite). The Communists' requisitioning of food leads to the peasants planting less and less. This, and the drought, mean that output in 1921 is less than half of what it had been in 1913. Disease accompanies the famine and there are reports of cannibalism. Only the lucky ones are brought food by the government's relief trains (above), and in two years about 5 million will die. Peasants who rebel in Tambov province are shot in batches and the sailors' revolt at Kronstadt naval base is brutally crushed. Food requisitioning is eventually dropped and free trade permitted, but this is only a temporary tactical retreat from the party's hard line.

1922

Lloyd George's post-war coalition government is replaced by Bonar Law's Conservative one. The Turks take Smyrna (Izmir) from the Greeks and Britain almost goes to war with Turkey when intervening between the two sides. Gandhi is jailed in India for civil disobedience. Mussolini forms Italy's first Fascist Government. The British Broadcasting Company (later Corporation) is formed. Tutankhamen's tomb is discovered by Howard Carter and Lord Carnarvon in Egypt. *Ulysses* by James Joyce and the poem *The Waste Land* by T. S. Eliot are published.

Irish Republican Army
men and youths put on a show of strength
in the streets of Dublin. Michael Collins signed
a treaty in December 1921 with the British, giving
birth to the Irish Free State, an independent entity
within the British Commonwealth, but this is not
enough for diehards like these, who are prepared
to plunge their country into civil war. In April they
seize Dublin's Four Courts until they are shelled out
by Free State troops using artillery lent by the British.
The fighting then moves to the countryside
with Collins himself being killed in an ambush
in County Cork in August. Peace only comes
in 1923 after 4,000 lives have been lost,
mainly Republicans.

1923

Stanley Baldwin becomes Britain's Conservative Prime Minister. All non-Fascist parties are banned in Italy. Germany suffers hyper-inflation, at its height running at 2,500 per cent a month. In November Hitler stages his abortive beerhall *Putsch* in Munich and is arrested. He uses his time in prison to write *Mein Kampf*. Mustafa Kemal declares Turkey a republic and begins its westernisation. An earthquake in Japan kills over 300,000 people. The cricketer Jack Hobbs scores his hundredth century and Suzanne Leglen wins Wimbledon for the fifth time.

Young German girls
lose their inhibitions (right), get back to Nature and in touch with their feelings as they dance naked in some northern forest. Isadora Duncan, the pioneering American-born promoter of dance, began something when she looked for inspiration to the figures on ancient Greek vases. The human body was not a matter for shame in the Classical World. The importance of the semi-conscious and of the instinctual is also becoming a commonplace in the wake of Freud and Jung, while the lure of the primitive is being felt in painting, sculpture and music. The search for physical and mental wellbeing through movement and dance is very much in the air in 1920s Europe, and is to be taken up and perverted by the Nazis with their 'Strength Through Joy' slogan in the 1930s. The true heir to Duncan is fellow-American dancer and choreographer Martha Graham (above).

1924

The first British Labour Government, led by Ramsay MacDonald, comes to power in January thanks to Liberal support, but is replaced by the Conservatives in October. Their victory owes a lot to the forged Zinoviev Letter purporting to be from Communist Russia to the Labour Party and encouraging it to stir up the workers and foment trouble. Lenin dies and Stalin soon becomes the most powerful figure in Russia, having Leon Trotsky denounced by the Communist Party in November. George Gershwin composes *Rhapsody in Blue* and E. M. Forster publishes *A Passage to India*.

A flying stunt.
Lillian Boyer defies death a thousand feet up (above). Air circuses featuring thrills like these are a new feature of the entertainment scene.

Surfing in California.
This night-time surfboarder (left) holds flares in either hand while clenching the tow rope in his teeth. The photograph was taken in the Pacific off Los Angeles, the home of the Hollywood film industry, and is typical of the publicity shots that the studios required of the stars – brash and flash, to catch the eye. Water-skiing is a later development, as is the craze for surfing proper on the ocean rollers.

1925

Britain returns to the Gold Standard under Winston Churchill, the Conservative Chancellor of the Exchequer. Hitler is out of prison and Mussolini assumes full dictatorial powers. General Chiang Kai-shek becomes the leader of the Kuomintang Party in China (see 1911, p.31) on the death of Sun Yat-sen. The *Exposition des Arts Decoratifs* in Paris gives birth to the Art Deco style. *The Great Gatsby* by F. Scott Fitzgerald, *Carry on Jeeves* by P. G. Wodehouse and *The Trial* by Franz Kafka are published. Charlie Chaplin stars in *The Gold Rush*.

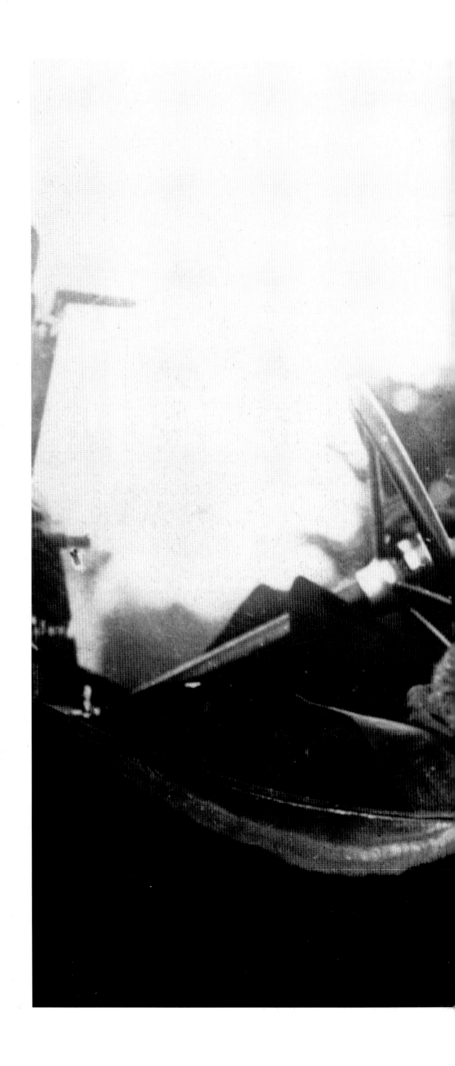

Mussolini with his pet lion cub.

Il Duce is notorious for his arrogant posturing, coining of empty slogans, and love of the grandiose gesture. A symbol of imperial strength such as the lion is bound to be an accessory close to his heart. It is easy to laugh at the Italian dictator's jowly portraits or pictures of him strutting and preening with his hands on his hips. In this one, the shape of his jaw seems echoed by that of his bowler. His regime may never reach the sub-human depths of the Nazis, but he is brutal and ruthless enough to political opponents or weaker states.

1926

The General Strike, called by the Trades Union Congress in support of already striking miners in May, lasts nine days, after 300,000 middle class volunteers rally to the British Government's call to keep the docks open and transport working. Joseph Pisludski becomes dictator of Poland after a military coup. John Logie Baird transmits the first television picture in London. Franz Kafka publishes *The Castle* and A. A. Milne *Winnie-the-Pooh*.

A glimpse of stocking?
These girls offer something more – no stockings at all (above).
Instead they have drawn charcoal designs on their legs, apparently in
homage to the grid-like pictures of the modern artist, Mondrian.

A bright 'eyedea'
from a 'bright young thing', as the 1920s flappers are also
known (opposite). Use an eyelash stencil alongside your eyebrow pencil.
If you can get your lashes to poke through the slits, then when you come
to apply your mascara you won't smudge your eyes. It's good for a laugh
even if you have forgotten to take off your fake fur coat first. Skirts are
short, hair is bobbed, powder compacts and lipsticks are as
much part of a girl's equipment as cloche hats
and long cigarette holders.

1927

In Britain the voting age for women is lowered to twenty-one. Civil war, involving Kuomintang forces, the armies of various independent warlords and the fledgling Communist Party, convulses China. Charles Lindbergh flies the Atlantic solo in his single-engined *Spirit of St Louis*, reaching Paris after thirty-three hours. Al Jolson's film *The Jazz Singer* signals the end of the road for silent movies.

Farming fun.
A cow being milked at King's Cross Station (top left); London girls with bundles of maize (top right), a new crop in Hertfordshire; a circus elephant ploughing (above left); and sheep being herded early one morning in Piccadilly (above right), on their way from keeping the grass down in Hyde Park to continue the job in Green Park, behind the railings.

In a Kent hopfield.
Two workers on stilts with bundles of twine which they will tie to the wires stretched horizontally between the poles (opposite). The hop bines or stalks will then grow up the twine. Hops give the bitter flavour to Britain's traditional beer. Whole families will come by train from the East End of London to strip the catkin-like fruits from the bines, sleeping in barns and sheds, and regarding the time away from their slums and tenements as a holiday outing, with pay.

1928

The age for receiving state pensions is lowered to sixty-five in Britain. Alexander Fleming discovers the antibacterial Penicillin mould. Mickey Mouse makes his first appearance in Walt Disney's cartoon film *Steamboat Willie*. Bert Hinkler makes the first solo flight from England to Australia, taking fifteen days, and an American–Australian team of four fly across the Pacific for the first time in a Fokker monoplane, arriving in Brisbane via Hawaii and Fiji ten days after taking off from the USA. Herbert Hoover succeeds Calvin Coolidge as US President. *Lady Chatterley's Lover* by D. H. Lawrence and *Decline and Fall* by Evelyn Waugh are published.

Amelia Earhart,
American aviatrix (above), in
Newfoundland just before she becomes the
first woman to fly the Atlantic, as a passenger.
In 1932 she is the first woman to fly it alone.
In 1937 she disappears on a flight
over the Pacific.

The icebreaker *Bear*
carrying the first of US Admiral
Richard Byrd's four Antarctic expeditions (left).
He has flown over the North Pole in 1926 and
will fly over the South Pole in 1929.

1929

Ramsay MacDonald forms a new Labour Government including the first woman Cabinet minister, Margaret Bondfield. British troops restore order after Arab–Jewish clashes in Jerusalem. In February Al Capone settles scores with Bugs Moran in Chicago's gangland war, killing seven of his O'Banion gang at the St Valentine's Day Massacre. In October the Wall Street Crash of the US Stock Market heralds the start of the world-wide Great Depression.

A Jacobean survival.
*Not a witches' coven, but elderly spinsters
living in the Hospital of the Holy and Undivided
Trinity at Castle Rising in Norfolk (left). These
almshouses and chapel were built in 1614 by Henry Howard,
Earl of Northampton, to house twelve such 'sisters' and a
'governess'. The long red cloaks bearing the Howard badge
and the pointed black hats are what have been worn since
the time of the charity's foundation. The Jacobean period
was an era when belief in witchcraft was potent, and our
image of a witch dates from then. (Above) The Chelsea
Pensioner's uniform isn't quite so old, though the Royal
Hospital there, where he lives, was founded by
Charles II. The ribbons show he is a supporter
of Chelsea FC.*

1930

By the end of this year there are over 4½ million unemployed in the USA and over 2 million in Britain. Soup kitchens and hunger marches become a regular part of the scene. The last Allied occupying troops leave the Rhineland and the Saar regions of Germany, where the Nazi Party polls 6½ million votes in the elections, making it the second biggest. Stalin imposes collectivism on agriculture in the USSR, killing many millions of 'kulaks' (better-off peasants) in the process. Gandhi launches his campaign of peaceful civil disobedience in British India. Amy Johnson flies solo to Australia from Britain, but the British R101 airship explodes at Beauvais in France on its first trip. The first sliced bread and frozen peas go on sale.

Women 'cracking' coal
down a mine, throwing out stone and slate, breaking up big lumps (above).
They wear goggles to protect their eyes from splinters. Judging by how clean they look,
this must be the start of the shift.

In a Kent coalfield,
three miners wear the minimum because of the heat down in the pit (opposite), *but no safety*
helmets or electric lamps. The photograph flatters the working conditions of many men, who had to hack,
doubled up, at narrow seams of coal. In 1925 the Government subsidy on coal was lifted, prices fell and
employers demanded wage cuts. The miners might have been earning good money – £4 a week – but
there were no pithead baths then; 1,300 were killed and 160,000 injured each year, not counting the
endemic lung disease caused by dust. So the cry was 'Not a minute on the day, not a penny
off the pay.' The General Strike in 1926 had really been to show solidarity with them.

1931

MacDonald's Labour administration is replaced by a National Government of Conservative, Liberal and Labour in August, and he leaves the Labour Party. Government spending is cut back and Britain comes off the Gold Standard. But unemployment is only half Germany's 5 million, while America's reaches 8¼ million. The Empire State Building is opened and Al Capone goes to prison for tax evasion, Spain becomes a republic and Japan seizes Manchuria from China. The films of *Dracula* and *Frankenstein* have their premieres.

Streetfighting in Germany

between rival bands of Communist and Nazi thugs
becomes a regular occurrence as they vie for power in the disturbed
atmosphere caused by the Great Depression. The German police need all
the new techniques and technology they can get to combat the threat to
civil peace. A bullet-proof alloy helmet and breastplate are demonstrated
(opposite), though it must be doubted whether the Luger pistol will
actually be fired. Police are also taught jujitsu unarmed combat
by a Swiss master and the lesson is filmed, perhaps to act as
a deterrent when shown later on the newsreels (above).

1932

Democratic President Franklin Roosevelt is elected by a landslide, pledging 'a new deal for the American people'. The Nazis double their representation in the Reichstag. Japan invades Shanghai in China. The Sydney Harbour Bridge is completed and the Mars Bar goes on sale. Aldous Huxley publishes his novel *Brave New World*.

Toy aeroplanes

make a brave show for the Christmas market (opposite).
In the real world the British Government may this year cancel its belief that
no great war need be expected for the next ten years, but Neville Chamberlain, the
Chancellor of the Exchequer, also introduces the lowest arms estimates between the
wars. The RAF has no streamlined monoplane fighters until Spitfires and Hurricanes arrive
in the second half of the decade. A small boy watches formations of bombers above
Duxford aerodrome in Cambridgeshire (above). The belief that 'the bomber will
always get through' can only be challenged once the new fighters are in
service, backed by the new radar.

1933

Hitler is elected Chancellor of Germany in January. The burning of the Reichstag building in February provides the excuse for the Nazis to start exercising dictatorial powers, throwing political opponents into the new concentration camps and persecuting the Jews. Roosevelt has his 'Hundred Days' of new initiatives to tackle the Depression. In Britain a £95 million slum clearance programme is announced. The Loch Ness Monster is 'sighted' and the film *King Kong* opens. Prohibition ends in the USA.

Hitler Youth
on the march (above). These indoctrinated and militarised adolescents have their equivalents in the Young Pioneers of the Soviet Union. A totalitarian state must control its peoples at every age.

Drying spaghetti
outside a pasta factory (left), a production method far from the automated, hygienic processes of today, but at least providing jobs for young men at a time when they are few and far between.

1934

A Socialist revolt in Austria is crushed and is shortly followed by an attempted Nazi coup, which fails. On the death of Field Marshal Hindenburg, Adolf Hitler becomes 'Führer', both President and Chancellor of Germany, having eliminated a potential rival, Ernst Röhm, head of the SA, and his henchmen in the 'Night of the Long Knives' in June. Mao Tse-tung and the Chinese Communist Party begin their Long March through the mountains to seek refuge in Shensi province where they can regroup. Bank robbers John Dillinger, and Bonnie and Clyde are killed in America. The first launderette opens and the board game Monopoly goes on sale.

RMS *Queen Mary*

*the day before she is launched into the Clyde at Glasgow (opposite).
She is not merely the world's largest ship, but also represents faith in a
future beyond the Depression, and a massive testimony to British design
and manufacturing skills when so many craftsmen are idle. The Art Deco
cocktail lounge can be seen fully fitted out and furnished (above right),
while the first-class dining-room (above left), though unfinished, has
a wall map of the Atlantic in position on which a series of lights
will chart the ship's progress.*

1935

Stanley Baldwin becomes Prime Minister of the National Government in Britain. Italy invades Ethiopia. The Saar area votes overwhelmingly to be reunited with Germany, where anti-Semitism is codified in the Nuremberg Laws. In the USA Roosevelt launches his second new deal with a massive programme of public works. The films *Top Hat* with Fred Astaire and Ginger Rogers, *A Night at the Opera* with the Marx Brothers and Alfred Hitchcock's *The Thirty-Nine Steps* with Robert Donat all open. Penguin paperbacks are launched in Britain.

The City of Steel.

Sheffield's factory chimneys speak of both pollution for those downwind and prosperity for the Yorkshire city itself (right). Germany is once more on the march so 'now thrive the armourers', in Shakespeare's words from Henry V, and there is work for the forges, mills and factories here, which will provide them with their basic material and vital finished components as well. Elsewhere in England, unemployment is still hurting, though down from its peak of 2³/₄ million in 1933. Will this man's appeal (above) get any response?

VAL DOONE

1936

George V dies but his successor, Edward VIII, abdicates before the end of the year on account of his love for an American divorcee, Wallis Simpson. The show trials of Stalin's fellow old Communist leaders are in full flow in Russia. Millions are being sent to the Siberian gulags. Spain descends into bitter civil war, the incumbent Republicans supported by Russia and General Franco's insurgent Nationalists by Italy and Germany. Germany reoccupies the Rhineland without any opposition from France or Britain. The Douglas DC-3 and the Supermarine Spitfire fly for the first time. Chiang Kai-shek declares war on Japan. Sergei Prokofiev's *Peter and the Wolf* is premiered and Margaret Mitchell's *Gone with the Wind* is published.

DOROTHEA LANGE

A migrant mother

*with two of her seven children at a farm workers' camp in
California (above). In 1935 extreme drought turned vast tracts of
the mid-West into a large dust bowl, with irreplaceable topsoil
being blown away. Families such as this trek westwards to
California to try to make a new life. But as John Steinbeck is to
make plain in his famous novel,* The Grapes of Wrath *(1939),
there is no promised land on the shores of the Pacific.*

A sharecropper's grave

*in Alabama (right), symbol of the abject poverty into
which much of American agriculture falls during the Depression.
Sharecroppers are tenants whose only contribution is their labour
and who receive a share of the resulting crop in payment, after
deductions for rent, seed, tools, etc, made by the landlord.
Nothing tells us whose grave this is.*

WALKER EVANS

1937

George VI is crowned in London, and Neville Chamberlain becomes Prime Minister on Baldwin's retirement. German aeroplanes bomb the town of Guernica in the Spanish Civil War which the Republicans are losing, in spite of the International Brigades of left-wing foreigners who fight for them. In China, Peking, Shanghai, Nanking and Hankow fall to the Japanese who carry out many atrocities. Walt Disney's first feature-length cartoon film, *Snow White and the Seven Dwarfs*, appears.

Dirty linen.

Nazi banners are washed before their next outing at yet another party rally. The Nazis are inspired designers and orchestrators of demonstrations and reviews, using symbols, colour, and sophisticated lighting to enhance the impact of the uniformed ranks of the army, SS, and other party organisations. The scale of these events submerges the individual in the mass hysteria of the people, whose eyes are inexorably drawn to the leadership and the Führer.

1938

Austria is annexed by Germany, and then the Sudetenland in Czechoslovakia, as France and Britain follow the policy of appeasing the rampant Hitler, in spite of the protests of Anthony Eden and Winston Churchill. In November nearly all Germany's synagogues are burnt and 7,000 Jewish shops destroyed in the orgy of violence known as *Kristallnacht*, the Night of Broken Glass. Thirty thousand Jews are arrested. The *Queen Elizabeth* is launched, even larger than the *Queen Mary*, and the first instant coffee, Nescafé, goes on sale.

Neville Chamberlain,
*the British Prime Minister (above), returns
from meeting Hitler on 1 October with the promise
of 'Peace in our Time', on a piece of paper he waves,
having bartered away the Sudetenland province of
Czechoslovakia for what turns out to be
only a breathing space.*

Sir Oswald Mosley
*surrounded by a bodyguard of British
Fascist blackshirt thugs in Bermondsey (right).
They march through London's East End in an attempt
to mobilise local anti-Semitic sentiment. Never with the
backing to call themselves a mass movement, they have
frequent encounters with Communist street fighters from
the opposite end of the political spectrum. Mosley
will spend the war in prison.*

1939

Britain and France recognise Franco's regime in Spain. Germany in effect takes over Czechoslovakia in March. Albania is invaded by Italy. Germany signs pacts with Italy and then Russia, then invades Poland on 1 September. Britain and France declare war on Germany. Poland is divided between Germany and Russia, which then invades Finland. A million British children are evacuated from towns and cities, but the expected bombs do not fall. This is the Phoney War when British bombers are sent out loaded with leaflets, not high explosives. *Stagecoach*, *Gone with the Wind* and *The Wizard of Oz* all open in the cinema.

Attention seeking.

*The ultimate fashion accessory,
flown in from Kenya, is taken shopping in London.
It seems a little tactless of its owner to have the fur of
another dead animal draped round her shoulders. Will
her pet cheetah be recycled into a handbag or pair of
shoes on its demise? By next year bunches of
bananas will only be a memory, not to return
to the shops until the late 1940s.*

1940

Germany invades Denmark and Norway, then the Benelux countries, followed by France, whose army is no match for the Wehrmacht's *Blitzkrieg*. Churchill becomes Prime Minister. Three hundred and thirty-seven thousand British and French troops escape from Dunkirk. The Battle of Britain is fought in the air over southern England and the Channel, and the London Blitz begins in September. The Italians, Germany's allies, are defeated by the British in North Africa and their fleet attacked from the air in Taranto harbour.

FRED MORLEY

Business as usual

is the slogan and ordinary Londoners are determined not to let the Blitz stop them leading their normal lives. A milk roundsman keeps the pints coming as he walks across the rubble (above).

A fire bomb

destroys Holland House, the Jacobean mansion in Kensington (right). The book-lined Long Gallery here was the great Whig stamping-ground in the early part of the 19th century, where the intelligentsia were entertained by Lord and Lady Holland. Insurance assessors scan the shelves the day after the raid. The switching of the Luftwaffe's bombing attacks from RAF aerodromes to London was a fundamental error by Goering, whatever it does to the fabric of the city.

1941

The Blitz on London is resumed and Coventry is badly bombed in April. Yugoslavia, Greece and Crete fall to the Germans. Hitler invades Russia in June and British forces are under pressure from Rommel in North Africa. The Japanese attack the US Pacific fleet at Pearl Harbor, then Germany and Italy declare war on the USA. Hong Kong falls to the Japanese. Leningrad is besieged and the Germans are on the outskirts of Moscow. The US Army takes delivery of the first Jeeps and Orson Welles' film *Citizen Kane* has its premiere.

WILLIAM VANDERSON

FRED RAMAGE

Mocking the monster.
A London boy has his Hitler carnival mask adjusted
by a friend (above left).

A wartime bride
leaves her bomb-damaged home for the church (above right),
her and her bridesmaid's outfits apparently making no compromise
to rationing or the surroundings.

The gas attacks
never come and the gas masks issued to everybody are
merely good for a laugh when worn by these two Southend
housewives in their pinnies and headscarves (opposite).

1942

The Japanese advance on all fronts in South-East Asia and the Pacific. Singapore falls in February and Burma is evacuated by the British, who also retreat before Rommel in North Africa. But then the US Navy administers a stunning blow to the Japanese fleet at Midway in June, the RAF mounts the first thousand-bomber raids on German cities and Montgomery precipitates Rommel's final long retreat at El Alamein in October. After the fall of the Crimea on the Black Sea, the German 6th Army is surrounded at Stalingrad on the Volga, and the drive towards the oil and mineral wealth of the Caucasus is halted. The economist William Beveridge publishes his report, which will become the blueprint for the post-war welfare state. The film *Casablanca* is premiered.

M. McNEILL

R. J. LEWIS, ISLE OF MAN

A pig may look at a King.
George VI inspects his farm in the grounds of Windsor Castle (left), *in a scene reminiscent of P. G. Wodehouse's Lord Emsworth and his champion pig, the Empress of Blandings. U-boats are sinking an Allied ship every four hours on average and the drive for every scrap of home-grown food is deadly serious. The piglet labelled Hitler* (above) *is the greediest of the litter.*

1943

The German army at Stalingrad surrenders. The US takes Guadalcanal in the Solomon Islands in February. In April German forces in North Africa surrender and the invasion of Sicily follows in July. The Allies land in Italy in September and Italy surrenders. Hamburg is bombed for five days running and 40,000 are killed. The remaining 60,000 Jews in the Warsaw Ghetto rise against the Germans. Four thousand are killed, the rest are taken to concentration camps. More than a million die from famine in Bengal.

Wargames.

The usual boyish fascination with guns (right) is given added point by the Washington, DC, high school cadets drilling in the background. US troops have landed in North Africa and will soon be in Sicily and Italy. War's reality is too much for this German (above), a loser in the Battle of Kursk on the central Russian plain (in July), the greatest tank battle in history.

1944

Monte Cassino monastery finally falls to the Allies in May and the road to Rome is open. It is taken on 4 June and the D-Day landings in Normandy follow two days later. General de Gaulle enters Paris on 26 August. The July Plot to assassinate Hitler narrowly fails. London is under a new threat from flying bombs – doodlebugs – and V2 rockets. Brussels is liberated on 5 September. The Russians are advancing on all fronts and take Bucharest, the capital of Romania. Belgrade, the capital of Yugoslavia, follows in October. The Germans counterattack in the Ardennes in December, unsuccessfully. The first Biro ballpoints go on sale in Argentina.

BERT HARDY

War effort.

Working on the nose cone of a Lancaster bomber (opposite),
each one of which represents a total investment of £120,000 including training its
five-man crew. One of the bombs it will carry is rolled across the shop floor by a nonchalant
munitions worker (above). Of the 16 million British women of working age, over 7 million do war
work, in uniform, industry or on the land. Their pay has risen by 80 per cent since 1938.

1945

Soviet forces enter Warsaw in January and Budapest in February, the same month that Dresden is needlessly flattened by Allied bombers, probably killing over 100,000. The full horror of the concentration camps is revealed in Poland and Germany. Some 7 million have entered them, mostly Jews; only 500,000 survive. Germany surrenders on 7 May. On 6 and 9 August atomic bombs are dropped on Hiroshima and Nagasaki in Japan, which surrenders on 14 August. Roosevelt has died on 12 April to be succeeded as US President by Harry Truman. In the British General Election, a big Labour victory means Clement Attlee replaces Winston Churchill as Prime Minister.

FRED RAMAGE

Russians and Americans
meet on the Elbe in April. All is fraternal greetings and accordion music in this carefully posed shot, but Stalin is determined that Berlin shall fall to his forces, not to GIs.

JACK ESTEN

Soldier's return,
that long-awaited moment when husband and wife are reunited.

REG SPELLER

V for Victory
finally in May and south Londoners celebrate
with an open-air banquet, as hoarded reserves can at
last be enjoyed.

1946

The United Nations General Assembly meets in London for the first time. Bread rationing is introduced in Britain, and the National Health Service is enacted. Although promised independence by Clement Attlee, India is racked by violence between the Hindu and Muslim communities. The latter demand their own independent state. There are also riots by Arabs in Jerusalem at the prospect of a Jewish state in Palestine. Chinese Communists declare war on the Kuomintang Nationalists. The first Vespa motor scooters go on sale in Italy.

FRANK HARRISON

Arms and the man.

Two technicians (above), both of whom have lost forearms, work on artificial arms at an exhibition in Britain, sponsored by the ministries of Health and Labour. Perhaps their civil servants derive particular satisfaction from the symmetry implicit in this.

War's aftermath.

A man waits for a tram in Vienna (opposite), his new artificial limb in his rucksack. Perhaps he has not yet learnt to use it with confidence, or he is taking it back for repair, or to have it altered so it fits his stump better.

1947

Britain suffers a bitter and prolonged winter, while the coalmines are nationalised, as will be steel, railways, power, long-distance road freight, civil aviation. Rationing gets worse and the only relief is provided by the marriage of Princess Elizabeth to Lieutenant Philip Mountbatten. India and Pakistan become independent in August. The Marshall Plan, for financial aid from the USA to help Europe recover, is proposed. Russia steps up its measures to impose Communist puppet regimes on the countries of Eastern and Central Europe. The Dead Sea Scrolls are discovered. The Kalashnikov AK-47 rifle is introduced to the Soviet army.

Zones, borders, barricades

feature largely in post-war European life.
A Dutch woman (left) bends down to kiss a grandchild she has not seen before through the fence dividing the mining town of Kerkrade between Holland and Germany. The multi-lingual sign warns that anyone climbing the wire is liable to be shot. The man with the brush is painting a border line in Berlin (above) so that police from the Russian-controlled area of the city will no longer have any excuse if they cross into the British zone in pursuit of black marketeers. Here is the Iron Curtain being made tangible.

1948

Burma becomes independent and Gandhi is assassinated. The Communists take over in Czechoslovakia. The State of Israel is proclaimed and comes under immediate attack from surrounding countries. When Russia blocks road and rail traffic into Berlin, an airlift of essential supplies begins from the West. Harry Truman wins the presidential election in America. The National Party wins the South African elections with a mandate to introduce Apartheid. The Morris Minor, Land Rover and Citroën 2 CV are launched, as are the first long-playing records, and the first transistor.

Defying death.
*Boys from the Gorbals in Glasgow use a cemetery
as an adventure playground, the only open area available to them,
symbolising the irrepressible upsurge of new life in spite of all
the killing that has gone on.*

BERT HARDY

SEYMOUR WALLERSTEIN

1949

Mao Tse-tung and the Chinese Communists defeat the Nationalists, whose remnants retreat to Taiwan. Holland recognises the independence of Indonesia. The Berlin blockade is lifted by the Soviets. Clothes and sweet rationing end in Britain, and the pound is devalued by 30 per cent. The German Federal Republic is formed in the west, and the German Democratic Republic in the east. The de Havilland Comet, the world's first jet airliner, makes its maiden flight. Orson Welles stars in *The Third Man*, and Ealing Studios produce *Kind Hearts and Coronets*, *Passport to Pimlico* and *Whisky Galore*. *Nineteen Eighty-Four* by George Orwell is published. His *Animal Farm* appeared in 1945.

Swoonlight Sinatra,
'the skinny kid with big ears' from Hoboken,
New Jersey, also simply known as 'The Voice',
rehearses at the London Palladium.

The Red menace.
New York State troopers gather round one
of their own (left), hit by a stone thrown by a
protester trying to stop a Paul Robeson concert. The
black Communist singer has just returned from a tour of
the Soviet Union. Anti-Communist feelings are running high
in the USA and the next year Republican Senator Joseph
McCarthy will whip them to a frenzy with his wild accus-
ations aimed at prominent Democrats and intellectuals.

1950

Attlee forms a new Labour Government after a very close General Election. Communist North Korea invades South Korea. United Nations forces, largely American, move to support South Korea and push the invaders back. Chinese forces come to the aid of the North Koreans, with Soviet 'advisers'. The Chinese invade Tibet. The first credit card, Diners' Club, comes into use in New York. *The Kon-Tiki Expedition*, by Thor Heyerdahl, is published.

Only in Japan.

Fifteen hundred young men (right), plunged in total darkness, try to find two prize-winning batons. This extraordinary lottery, held as part of a cultural festival, is briefly illuminated by the photographer's flash. More prosaically, these girls manufacturing machine parts (above) are helping Japanese industry back on its feet, ready for the huge leap forward it is to take in the 1950s.

1951

The Festival of Britain is mounted in London, a hundred years after the Great Exhibition held in the Crystal Palace in 1851. The Conservatives win the General Election and Churchill is back in power. Soviet spies, Burgess and Maclean, flee to Russia. Fighting goes on in Korea but General MacArthur is relieved of his command after first threatening to drop an atomic bomb, then to invade China. British forces occupy the Suez Canal Zone in Egypt. J. D. Salinger's novel, *The Catcher in the Rye*, is published.

Station sunlight
*catches two British soldiers in its beams at Liverpool Street,
London's busiest terminus (opposite). Architecturally, its red-brick
Gothic could not be in greater contrast to the Dome of Discovery, the
most original of the buildings erected for the Festival of Britain on
London's South Bank (above). Crowds queue here for the opening
ceremony of the Festival, brainchild of the Labour politician Herbert
Morrison, whose grandson Peter Mandelson will be responsible
for the Millennium Dome, a few miles down the river
and fifty years on (see 1999, p. 206).*

1952

King George VI dies of lung cancer. Republican Dwight Eisenhower ceases being Supreme Commander of Allied Forces and is elected US President. The Malayan Emergency, caused by Communist terrorists, is at its height. There are anti-British riots in Egypt and King Farouk abdicates. The Mau Mau Emergency begins in Kenya, with attacks on white settlers and the terrorising of much of the African population. Britain explodes its first atomic bomb, and the USA its first hydrogen bomb. *The Diary of Anne Frank* is published.

BERT HARDY

Billy Butlin

set up his first holiday camp at Skegness on the Lincolnshire coast in 1936,
his motto a quotation from Shakespeare: 'Our true intent is all for your delight.'
For the 'redcoat' camp assistants this sometimes means parading in swimsuits and Marilyn Monroe
masks (opposite), and sometimes rolling up a contestant's long johns in a knobbly knee
competition (above). However, opera and Shakespeare are also provided. Butlin built three
camps during the war, partly paid for by the government which housed troops in them.
With foreign holidays still expensive rarities, he is doing a roaring trade.

1953

Queen Elizabeth is crowned and on the same day, 2 June, the news comes through of the first ascent of Mount Everest by the British team. The Korean War ends, but in Vietnam the French are fighting guerrillas from the north led by Ho Chi Minh. Soviet forces suppress a revolt in East Berlin, then Stalin dies. *The Mousetrap* by Agatha Christie opens, *Under Milk Wood* by Dylan Thomas is broadcast and Ian Fleming publishes his first James Bond novel, *Casino Royale*. British scientists discover the structure of DNA, the key to heredity.

Crown, orb and sceptre.
*The Queen smiles, perhaps with relief (above), as
she carries the symbols of sovereignty into Buckingham Palace
after her Coronation. Outside Westminster Abbey after the
ceremony peers hurry across the road in the rain (right), on
their way to the House of Lords where they can disrobe
and doff their coronets.*

1954

Comet airliners are crashing for no apparent reason and have to be withdrawn. This gives the US aeronautical industry its chance, as the Boeing 707 makes its maiden flight. Roger Bannister runs the first four-minute mile. Rationing ends in Britain after fourteen years. The French withdraw from Vietnam and the country is divided, with the northern half under the Communists in Hanoi. French rule is also coming under attack in Algeria. The Salk polio vaccine goes on trial. *Lucky Jim* by Kingsley Amis, *Lord of the Flies* by William Golding and *The Lord of the Rings* by J. R. R. Tolkien are published.

BERT HARDY

Teddy Boys
ape the Edwardian gentlemen with fancy waistcoats and
velvet collars (opposite). *Greased hair and crêpe-soled brothel creepers complete the*
outfit. The girls sucking on their milkshakes (above left) *are the first butterflies to escape*
the drab post-war chrysalis, heralding a new era of teenage
affluence and independence.

Chelsea at night.
A young couple have also escaped from some vaguely artistic party,
to embrace among the dustbins (above right).

1955

Anthony Eden replaces Churchill as Prime Minister. Unrest between Greek and Turkish communities in Cyprus reaches new heights. EOKA, the Greek Cypriot terrorist organisation, tries by bomb and murder to bring about union with Greece. Princess Margaret does not marry Peter Townsend. Martin Luther King leads bus boycotts in Montgomery, Alabama. Bill Haley's 'Rock Around the Clock' tops the charts in the USA and Britain. Fans riot at an Elvis Presley concert, and Chuck Berry's first single, 'Maybelline', reaches the Top 10.

Jazz, skiffle and pop.
*The first stirrings of the popular music revolution,
heavily influenced by American models, are abroad. A fifteen-year-old
John Lennon plays with his skiffle group, the Quarrymen (above),
complete with a bass made out of an old tea chest, a broom
handle and a piece of string. A very young Shirley Bassey (opposite)
poses in her home in the Tiger Bay area of Cardiff.*

JOHN PRATT

THURSTON HOPKINS

1956

The Greek Cypriot leader, Archbishop Makarios, is deported by the British, while unrest and killings continue on the island. Nikita Khrushchev, the Soviet leader, attacks each stage of Stalin's career in a speech to the 20th Party Congress. Nasser effectively nationalises the Suez Canal. Britain and France, in secret collusion with Israel, go to war with Egypt, but do not have US backing so are soon forced to withdraw. At the same moment, partly inspired by Krushchev's speech, the Hungarians rise up against the Communist regime in their country, and are then sub-dued by Soviet tanks. John Osborne's play, *Look Back in Anger,* opens in London.

A new toothpaste
gets a pythonesque launch.
Messerschmitt bubble cars, looking like
sawn-off cockpits from some of the designer's
earlier products, are made even more bizarre by
the boxes teed up above them. The car on the
left has its roof tipped over, showing how
the driver gains entry.

1957

Anthony Eden resigns as a result of the Suez debacle and is succeeded as Prime Minister by Harold Macmillan. The Gold Coast (Ghana) and the Malayan Federation become independent. The Wolfenden Report on homosexual offences and prostitution is published. In Little Rock, Arkansas, nine black pupils challenge the segregation in schools which applies there and throughout the southern United States, though ruled unconstitutional by the Supreme Court in 1954. They are kept out first by State Troopers under orders from the Governor, then by a white mob, until 1,000 paratroopers sent by President Eisenhower escort them to school. The first parking meters come to London and *Dr Zhivago* by Boris Pasternak is published.

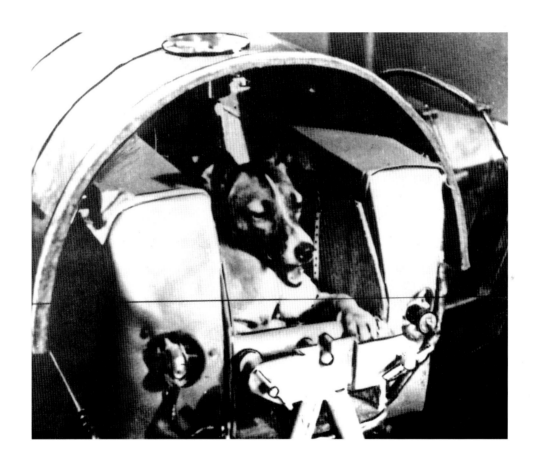

Animals in science.
Laboratory rabbits are subjected to a new drug
to see whether it might be suitable for use by humans (left).
In October the Russians launch the first satellite into space.
A month later Sputnik II takes off, crewed by Laika the dog (above). *After*
a week in orbit she dies when her oxygen supply runs out. By 1961 the
Russians will be able to launch dogs and bring them back, paving
the way for the first manned spaceflight that year.

1958

The European Economic Community is formed, consisting of France, Germany, Italy and the Benelux countries. The Campaign for Nuclear Disarmament is launched in Britain. The King of Iraq is toppled in a coup. US marines are sent to the Lebanon and British troops to Jordan to support incumbent governments against the threat of anti-Western Arab nationalism. Violence escalates in Cyprus. General de Gaulle is made French Prime Minister in the hope he can deal with the crisis in Algeria. Mao Tse-tung attempts to transform the Chinese economy with his Great Leap Forward which, by 1962, results in 30 million dead. Eight Manchester United footballers are killed in an air crash at Munich. The Lego children's building brick is launched and the integrated circuit is invented.

Race riots

in Notting Hill, London. Many immigrants from the Caribbean
have come to live in this area of North Kensington and racist taunts from white
youths lead to confrontations, then bottle and petrol bomb throwing. Within a week nine
youths have been jailed for four years each for attacking blacks. A man is searched for
weapons (opposite), *while the police sergeant restrains his right hand and arm.*
Youths and children run through the streets (above), *part of a*
2,000-strong mob, attacking black houses.

1959

Makarios is elected President of an independent Cyprus with a Turkish Vice-President. The Dalai Lama flees to India in the face of Chinese persecution in Tibet. De Gaulle becomes President of France. The first hovercraft, invented in Britain, flies the Channel. The first xerox copying machine goes on sale, as does the Morris Mini car. Laurie Lee's *Cider With Rosie* is published, and William Burroughs' *The Naked Lunch*.

DOROTHY SPOONER

The television invasion.

*By now two-thirds of British homes have one,
though not, it appears, this house in Wembley (opposite). So the
girls have come round with their portable set, though it takes two to carry
it. More sensibly the man has brought a bottle. The proprietor of this
soda fountain in Indiana knows how to get the kids into his store and
keep them there – install a TV (above).*

1960

Harold Macmillan, touring Africa, makes his 'Winds of Change' speech. At a black protest meeting at Sharpeville in South Africa against Apartheid laws, sixty-seven people are shot dead by the police. The Congo is hastily given independence by Belgium and plunges into law-lessness. Julius Nyerere becomes Tanganyika's first Chief Minister. An American U-2 spy plane is shot down over Russia. White settlers in Algeria revolt because they suspect de Gaulle will give the country its independence. John F. Kennedy is elected US President. Alfred Hitchcock's film *Psycho* and Robert Bolt's play *A Man For All Seasons* are premiered.

Cuba Libre,
a cocktail of rum and Coca-Cola, epitomises the good
American–Cuban relations now, spelt out on the billboard at Miami in
Florida by the country's new ruler (left). Castro has ousted the corrupt Batîstá
regime with the encouragement of the USA. But his wholesale nationalisations
and flirtations with the Communist bloc soon sour things. The abortive Bay of Pigs
invasion, masterminded by the CIA, follows in 1961, then the missile crisis in
1962. Cuba has always supplied some of America's best baseball players and here
Castro opens a tournament in Havana (above).

1961

Britain applies for membership of the EEC while Sierra Leone becomes independent from her. Civil war breaks out in the Portuguese colony of Angola. French generals in Algeria mount an abortive revolt against de Gaulle's plans to give it independence. The Berlin Wall is erected to stem the haemorrhage after 2.6 million of the best and brightest have fled from East Germany since 1946. Soviet cosmonaut Yuri Gagarin is the first man in space. The contraceptive pill becomes available. The twist is the latest dance craze. The E-type Jaguar is launched and *Beyond The Fringe* opens in London.

Winkle picker
toes and stiletto heels (above) – one of the earliest of the many fashions that are to be such a feature of the Swinging Sixties. The traditional way to extract the occupant from a winkle shell is with a pin. This trend horrifies the medical profession who say women are storing up problems for their feet later on.

The Berlin Wall
is up and sightseers use the luggage rack on top of a bus as a grandstand to look at the Eastern Sector of the city (left).

1962

Jamaica, Trinidad, and Uganda become independent from Britain, and Algeria from France. Russia starts shipping missiles to Cuba but, confronted by President Kennedy, Khrushchev agrees to remove them. John Glenn is the first US astronaut, though his autopilot malfunctions and his heat shield is in danger of falling off. Marilyn Monroe dies and The Beatles break through to the big time. *One Day In The Life of Ivan Denisovich* by Alexander Solzhenitsyn is published.

Tower blocks
*of flats for the workers are a phenomenon
all over Europe, east and west. The vistas in the
Gorbals area of Glasgow (left) and Sarcelles, France
(above), are almost interchangeable. These high-rises
appeal to the planners and local politicians since they are
quick and cheap to build out of prefabricated units. This
is the 'scientific' way forward advocated by the gurus of
the Modern Movement in architecture. But they destroy
street life and community spirit, force dependence on
erratic lifts, and often start to leak and decay at an
alarming rate. Many will turn into slums as bad
as the terraces and tenements they replace.*

ALBERT McCABE

1963

De Gaulle blocks Britain's entry to the EEC, while Kenya and Nigeria become independent. Kim Philby is revealed as a Soviet spy. Sir Alec Douglas-Home succeeds Harold Macmillan as Prime Minister. The Civil Rights campaign in the USA reaches a new intensity, with weeks of rioting in Birmingham, Alabama and a march of more than 200,000 supporters on Washington. Kennedy is shot dead in Dallas, Texas, and Lyndon Johnson becomes President. The assassin, Lee Harvey Oswald, is shot dead two days later by Jack Ruby, a nightclub owner with a criminal record. Bob Dylan shares the charts with The Beatles. Push-button telephones and television instant replays are introduced.

R. LANCASTER

Brigitte Bardot,
the French film star who set male hearts palpitating in the 1950s, is still at it in the 1960s.

The Profumo Affair
sends the media into a feeding frenzy; its photographers are seen here surrounding the two girls at the centre of the story (opposite), Christine Keeler (dark) and Mandy Rice-Davies (blonde). John Profumo, Secretary of State for War, has been infatuated with Keeler, but unfortunately for him, she has been sharing her favours with Captain Eugene Ivanov of the Soviet embassy. Mandy Rice-Davies has only been the mistress of Peter Rackham, the notorious slum landlord. Profumo denies involvement, is found out, and forced to resign. Macmillan has had enough and in turn resigns as Prime Minister.

1964

Malawi (Nyasaland), Zambia (Northern Rhodesia) and Malta become independent of Britain. Labour wins the General Election and Harold Wilson becomes Prime Minister with a majority of five seats. Khrushchev is ousted from power in the Kremlin and replaced by Leonid Brezhnev. America involvement in Vietnam escalates. Nelson Mandela is jailed for life in South Africa.

The Tokyo Olympics
throws up the usual crop of sensations, including the performance, and appearance, of Tamara Press of Russia (above), who breaks the record for the women's shot put.

Cassius Clay,
seven-to-one outsider, celebrates winning the world heavyweight boxing title from Sonny Liston (opposite). He runs round the ring proclaiming, 'I am the greatest!' and before the contest promised to 'float like a butterfly and sting like a bee'. He is shortly to change his name to Muhammad Ali, on his conversion to Islam.

1965

Winston Churchill dies. Ian Smith's white government in Southern Rhodesia unilaterally declares independence. A stable regime under General Mobutu is set up in Zaire (Congo). American planes bomb North Vietnam and by August there are 125,000 US soldiers deployed in South Vietnam. Black civil rights activities grow in the United States, backed by new legislation. The drive for black voter registration is centred on Selma, Alabama. Martin Luther King leads a march of 25,000 from there to the state capital, Montgomery. There is race rioting at Watts in Los Angeles, with thirty-four people killed. The film *The Sound of Music* has its premiere.

DON McCULLIN

An English Fascist

at a Trafalgar Square meeting. Her hatred may be real enough, but she will have to learn to get her swastika the other way round before she becomes a true heir to the Nazis (above).

White Supremacist

Ku Klux Klansmen may look ridiculous in their hoods and white sheets, with their grand Goblin, Great Titan and Kleagle titles, but the violence they dish out to 'uppity niggers' in the southern states of America is real enough. Their lynchings, fire bombings and beatings may have reached a peak in the 1920s but the organisation continues, as this photo of a Klan mother and baby (also hooded) in South Carolina testifies (opposite). Klan hatred encompasses Roman Catholics and Jews as well as blacks.

1966

Labour wins a landslide victory in the British General Election. England wins the Football World Cup, defeating West Germany in the final at Wembley. The Moors Murderers, Ian Brady and Myra Hindley, are jailed for life. Freddie Laker takes on the airline giants, offering a cheap transatlantic service. Mao Tse-tung announces the Cultural Revolution, setting the youth of China against their elders and unleashing years of chaos and persecution. Florence is flooded and many works of art are damaged. Mrs Indira Gandhi becomes Prime Minister of India.

A slag heap

by the Welsh village of Aberfan, near Merthyr Tydfil, collapses on the local school. Heavy rain has made it unstable and it engulfs 147, mostly children. Almost an entire generation of the village is dead, under 2 million tons of mine waste and sludge. If it had happened a few hours later, the school would have been empty, closed for half-term. Some of the 2,000 rescue workers are outlined against the night sky by floodlights.

1967

Britain withdraws from Aden and applies for membership of the EEC for a second time, and de Gaulle again exercises France's veto. The Abortion Act is passed, and the pound is devalued by 15 per cent. Israel routs Egypt, Jordan and Syria in the Six-day War, after aggressive moves by Colonel Nasser. Most of the West Bank of the Jordan, the old city of Jerusalem and the Golan Heights fall to Israel. In Greece, the army seizes power and the regime of the Colonels begins. During ground testing of the first Apollo spacecraft three US astronauts are burnt to death. The cult revolutionary hero Che Guevara is killed in Bolivia and Dr Christiaan Barnard carries out the first successful heart transplant in South Africa. In Detroit there are four days of race riots and forty dead; for the hippies in Haight-Ashbury, San Francisco, the Summer of Love passes in a haze of pot and LSD.

The dog breeders'
*year climaxes at Cruft's Show in London.
Here two chihuahua owners exchange pleasantries
before they meet in the ring (right), the one on the right
proving an observable fact of life: that very small dogs
often have very large owners. The dog in the wig (above)
seems to be looking with a mixture of pity
and disgust at whoever has perpetrated such
an indignity on it.*

1968

After US offensives in 1966 and 1967 and with half a million US troops in Vietnam, the Viet Cong launch their Tet Offensive, overrunning Hué and even capturing the US embassy in Saigon for a few hours. Viet Cong casualties are horrendous but US opinion starts to turn against the war. Republican Richard Nixon is elected US President. Robert Kennedy and Martin Luther King are assassinated. Alexander Dubcek, new leader of Czechoslovakia, brings in liberal measures, which in turn bring in Soviet tanks to enforce a crackdown. US astronauts orbit the Moon while Stanley Kubrick's *2001: A Space Odyssey* is premiered.

Students on the streets
in Paris in May (above), responding to police tear gas with paving stones. The rioting by left-wingers is large scale, but they never get the support of the workers which would turn their protest into a threat.

Ibo women and children
are guarded by a Nigerian soldier dangling a hand grenade by its release pin (opposite). The civil war in Nigeria began in 1967 when the eastern part of the country split off under its leader, Colonel Ojukwu, and declared itself the Independent Republic of Biafra. The Ibos of Biafra met with success at first, but by now Nigerian forces have gained the upper hand. A big international aid operation is being mounted to fly in supplies to the beleaguered Biafrans.

1969

Troops are sent into Northern Ireland to try and stem sectarian violence sparked by Protestant attacks on Catholic civil rights marchers. Neil Armstrong and Buzz Aldrin become the first men on the Moon. The Franco-British supersonic jet airliner Concorde has its first flight, as does the Boeing 747 jumbo jet. France formally withdraws from NATO, Georges Pompidou becomes French President and Willi Brandt becomes German Chancellor. Colonel Gadaffi seizes power in Libya. The Woodstock pop festival takes place in the USA while BBC TV shows Kenneth Clark's *Civilisation* series and *Monty Python's Flying Circus*.

Flower people,
flower power are phrases on people's lips. Flower petals have been arranged round a model's eyes to give a startling look (opposite), *like the 'sun' hairstyle displayed round the face of the decade, the model Jean Shrimpton* (above). *In the fashion world, effects must go to extremes to attract attention, among all the exposed flesh, beautiful people and psychedelia.*

1970

Edward Heath leads the Conservatives to victory in the General Election. Student anti-war demonstrators are shot dead at Kent State University, Ohio. The USA bombs Cambodia and Laos as the Vietnam War spreads. Palestinian terrorists blow up three British, Swiss and American hijacked airliners in Jordan. Nasser and de Gaulle die, as do Janis Joplin and Jimi Hendrix. The crew of Apollo 13 survive an explosion in space, using the small landing module engines to steer back to earth. The floppy disk takes over from magnetic tape as the computer's means of storing information.

John Lennon's and Yoko Ono's
Christmas message (above) *hasn't got through to these Viet Cong soldiers, 'somewhere in South Vietnam'* (opposite), *photographed by an East European journalist. They are armed with AK-47s and the one on the right is pulling out the release pin of a grenade with his teeth. It is the USA's determination to continue the Vietnam War that is being eroded by the peace protesters.*

Decimal currency is introduced in Britain. The introduction of internment without trial for suspected terrorists is mishandled in Northern Ireland. Idi Amin comes to power in Uganda. Civil war breaks out in East Pakistan and 7 million flee over the border to India. US Lieutenant Calley is convicted of the massacre of civilians at the Vietnamese village of My Lai in 1969. US astronauts drive on the Moon in a special buggy. Three Russians die returning from space. Hot pants are the new fashion, and *The French Connection* and *A Clockwork Orange* the new films.

FRANK BARRETT

The Miss World Contest,
outside and inside the Albert Hall. Miss Brazil (above)
wears the crown she has just won, with the runners-up,
Miss Britain (left) and Miss Portugal (right). Outside, women's libbers
protest at what they regard as the voyeuristic exploitation of the meat
market taking place within. One of them has donned the uniform of a
'sex object', though it is too cold to dispense with her sheepskin
Afghan coat, a garment redolent of this era (opposite).

CHRIS DJUKANOVIC

1972

Thirteen civilians are killed in Londonderry on Bloody Sunday when paratroopers open fire during an anti-internment march. The Northern Irish Parliament at Stormont is suspended and direct rule by Westminster begins. A British miners' strike results in a three-day week being imposed. After a war between India and Pakistan, the new state of Bangladesh is formed from what was East Pakistan. Idi Amin expels the Asians from Uganda and many come to Britain. Nine Israeli athletes taken hostage at the Munich Olympics die in a gun battle between Palestinian terrorists and German police. The Baader–Meinhof terrorist gang are arrested in Germany. President Nixon visits China, bombs North Vietnam, and signs the Strategic Arms Limitation Agreement with Russia. The pocket calculator appears.

PAUL DELMA

Two politicians,

Margaret Thatcher, Conservative Minister of Education and Science (above), with a picture of Edward Heath, the man she is to displace from the leadership of her party. She is on the way up, while 'Tricky Dicky' Nixon is on the way down. Seen here electioneering in Ohio (right), he may win a second term, but the Watergate Affair has broken and the full scope of his involvement will soon be revealed.

1973

Britain, Ireland and Denmark join the EEC. Egypt and Syria launch a surprise attack on Israel, the Yom Kippur War. Israel absorbs the attack but oil prices rise by 70 per cent. UK miners start an over-time ban and there is another three-day week as well as a 50 mph speed limit. The Vietnam peace treaty is signed in Paris. The Spanish Prime Minister is assassinated by Basque terrorists. Socialist President Allende of Chile is ousted by General Pinochet. Glam rock is this year's style in pop music, with androgynous male singers in make-up.

DAVID NEWELL SMITH

In Brussels,
*the two prime movers of Britain's entry to the
EEC, Harold Macmillan and Edward Heath (above),
look suitably pensive after the momentous step.*

Value Added Tax
*must replace purchase tax now Britain is in the
EEC and a local photographer arranges that the VAT
headquarters in Southend spell out the initials by
pulling down some of the blinds (left).*

RON CASE

155

1974

Edward Heath calls a General Election against a background of unprecedented trades union unrest. Labour forms a minority government. An attempt at power sharing between Catholics and Protestants in Northern Ireland collapses in the face of a strike fomented by hard-line Protestants. The IRA mount a bombing campaign in mainland Britain, culminating with twenty-one killed in two Birmingham pubs. Labour gains a small majority in a second Election. Nixon resigns as President as a result of the Watergate scandal and is succeeded by Gerald Ford. Suspecting a Greek coup there, Turkey invades Cyprus and occupies part of the island. A coup in Portugal ousts its right-wing government. Lord Lucan vanishes and Alexander Solzhenitsyn is expelled from Russia.

MALCOLM CLARKE

Foreign holidays
for all is the cry and Spanish hoteliers are out to make
the most of it, despoiling their Mediterranean coast with monotonous
concrete high rises, like this one in Benidorm (opposite), to cater for the
package tourists. The French air traffic controllers aren't far behind them,
regularly striking for higher wages at the peak of the holiday
season and inflicting delays on thousands of passengers,
like these at Heathrow (above).

MAURICE HIBBERD

1975

Britain votes in a referendum to stay in the EEC. Margaret Thatcher becomes leader of the Conservative Party. Portugal finally withdraws from Angola, where civil war continues, as it does in the Lebanon. General Franco, the Spanish dictator, dies and Juan Carlos becomes King of Spain. The Communist North Vietnamese seize South Vietnam and the Communist Khmer Rouge seize Cambodia.

STEVE BENBOW

Emotive issues.

*A seal covered in oil lies on a Welsh beach where
a slick has come ashore* (above left). *A child carries a slogan protesting at
a chemical company using animals in its experiments* (above right).

Dutch elm disease

*strikes in Richmond Park and infected trees
are marked with a white cross before they are felled* (opposite). *It is in
English hedgerows, those that the farmers are not ripping out, that the
absence of elms will be most noticed.*

1976

Harold Wilson hands over the premiership, and an acute sterling crisis, to James Callaghan. Britain and Europe suffer a prolonged drought. Both Chou En-lai and Mao Tse-tung die, and in the subsequent power struggle the Gang of Four, including Mao's widow, are arrested. Democrat peanut farmer Jimmy Carter becomes US President. Israeli commandos release over 100 hijacked airline passengers from Palestinian terrorists at Entebbe airport in Uganda.

'A crime against the conscience and dignity of mankind'
is how the UN Security Council condemns South Africa's Apartheid laws in this, the year of the Soweto killings. These two pictures point up the blinkered idiocy of the regime. The demand that all teaching in black secondary schools should be in Afrikaans, the language of the Boers, triggers the rioting in the country's largest township near Johannesburg, which leaves 100 dead.

THE DIVISIONAL COUNCIL OF THE CAPE

WHITE AREA

BY ORDER SECRETARY

DIE AFDELINGSRAAD VAN DIE KAAP

BLANKE GEBIED

OP LAS SEKRETARIS

MAX SCHNEIDER

1977

The Grunwick photograph processing plant in London, where workers have been sacked, is picketed for a year, sometimes by eighteen thousand people, becoming the focal point for labour unrest and radical agitation. Eight hundred thousand 'boat people' flee Vietnam. Fighting with local independence movements escalates in Rhodesia. President Bhutto of Pakistan is ousted by a military coup led by General Zia ul-Haq. A Palestinian airliner hijack at Mogadishu is foiled by a German anti-terrorist squad. Black leader Steve Biko is murdered while in South African police custody. SF takes over Hollywood with *Star Wars* and *Close Encounters of the Third Kind*.

The Punk Rockers

arrive (right), a generation young enough and ignorant enough to appropriate a deeply reviled symbol as some sort of fashion accessory, combining it with lengths of chain and safety pins which hint at bondage and masochism. Maybe the original punks thought to convey their nihilism and contempt for the Establishment by using swastikas, but most who wear their depressing uniform are simply following the trend. This one softens the offensiveness of his outfit by adding a Union Jack, a gesture perhaps to the Jubilee, celebrating the Queen's twenty-five years on the throne, like Mr Fred English's flag in the picture above.

CHRIS MOORHOUSE

1978

Britain has 2 million unemployed and Jim Callaghan's pay freeze crumbles before the assault of organised labour. A pro-Communist regime emerges in Afghanistan and there is much opposition to the rule of the Shah in Iran. A former Italian Prime Minister, Aldo Moro, is kidnapped and killed by Red Brigade terrorists. Deng Xiaoping emerges as the new ruler of China, and starts to bring an end to Maoist excesses and to liberalise the economy. A Polish Pope, John Paul II, is elected. Egypt and Israel sign a peace treaty at Camp David, Maryland. The first 'test-tube baby' is born.

FRANK BARRETT

The Notting Hill Carnival,
and a policeman poses with some costumed dancers from the parade. This annual event at the August Bank Holiday weekend has grown over the years to become by far the biggest of its kind in the country, attracting hundreds of thousands to listen to the rock and steel bands, drink rum, eat goat, and savour the herbal fragrances in the air.

1979

A public-sector workers' strike brings a 'Winter of Discontent' to Britain with schools closed, bodies unburied, rubbish uncollected. Labour falls and Margaret Thatcher comes to power. The Lancaster House Conference in London arranges for elections to be held in Zimbabwe (formerly Southern Rhodesia). The Shah flees Iran and Islamic fundamentalist Ayatollah Khomeini comes to power. Russia invades Afghanistan. Idi Amin is ousted from Uganda and the rule of Pol Pot and the Khmer Rouge ends in Cambodia, with millions dead. The USA suffers its worst nuclear scare at Three Mile Island power station, Pennsylvania.

Dirty protest.
A cell at the Maze Prison in Belfast decorated by its IRA occupant with his own excrement in protest at not being granted political status (right). He will also be refusing to wash or to wear prison clothing, making do with a blanket instead. A typical 'political' act of the IRA is to plant a bomb on Lord Mountbatten's boat in Sligo, killing him and two boys, and badly wounding three relatives. His coffin is carried by naval ratings (above).

1980

A minority Arab group seizes the Iranian Embassy in London, which is then stormed by the SAS. British inflation reaches 21.8 per cent. Robert Mugabe is elected the first Prime Minister of Zimbabwe. American hostages are held by revolutionary Iranian students in the Teheran Embassy. A US special forces rescue attempt ends in disaster. Iraq invades Iran. A bomb blast in Bologna, the work of a neo-Fascist group, kills seventy-six. The Solidarity Movement emerges in Poland, led by Lech Walesa. Ronald Reagan wins the US Presidency. Smallpox is officially declared eradicated from the Earth.

A Guardian Angel

rides on a New York subway train covered in graffiti, offering protection from muggers and pickpockets (right). The volunteer body to which he belongs is keen to avoid the label of vigilante, but its existence is a testimony to the failure of the forces of law and order to keep the lid on New York's violence and crime. The city has many ideal breeding grounds for these, like the slums known as Hell's Kitchen in Manhattan (above).

1981

Mrs Thatcher slashes public spending and raises indirect taxation, while unemployment goes above 13 per cent. Labour chooses left-winger Michael Foot as its leader and four prominent members leave to form the Social Democrat Party. There is rioting in Brixton, Southall and Toxteth, Liverpool. IRA hunger striker Bobby Sands dies in jail in Belfast. President Sadat of Egypt is murdered by Islamic fundamentalists. Ronald Reagan and the Pope survive assassination attempts. The US hostages from the Teheran Embassy are released. An attempted right-wing coup in Spain is foiled by King Juan Carlos. IBM introduces a desktop computer to sell alongside Apple's. Aids is officially recognised as a world threat.

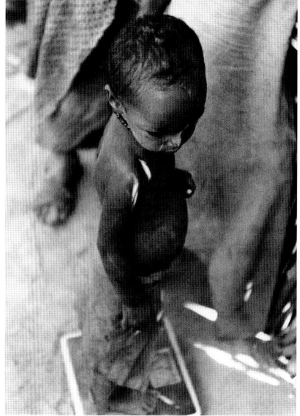

ARTHUR JONES

A gust of wind

helpfully arranges Princess Diana's long veil
as she pauses to look back (left), at the foot of the steps outside
St Paul's Cathedral, before her wedding. This 19-year-old former
kindergarten assistant is being watched by 1.2 billion as she does
so. Later, just before her divorce from the Prince of Wales, she is
to look back again and ruefully calls hers 'a crowded marriage'.
One of her best legacies is the compassion she displays towards
the sick, the old, and victims worldwide, like this Somali child
displaced from home by war and famine (above).

1982

Argentina invades the Falklands on 2 April; British troops land on 22 May and enter Port Stanley on 14 June. IRA bombs in Hyde Park and Regent's Park kill soldiers. Israel invades the Lebanon to root out the Palestine Liberation Organisation there after the Israeli ambassador in London is killed. Lebanese allies of Israel massacre Palestinians in Sabra and Chatila camps. Solidarity is outlawed in Poland. Yuri Andropov takes over as Russia's ruler on the death of Leonid Brezhnev.

Argentinian armour

lined up in Port Stanley after the invasion of the Falkland Islands (right). *Britain responds immediately to this desperate ploy by the struggling military dictatorship of General Galtieri, by sending a naval task force.* (Above) *Royal marine commandos wait on the deck of the aircraft carrier HMS* Hermes *before being airlifted ashore by helicopter.*

RAPHAEL WOLLMANN

1983

The Conservatives win the General Election and Neil Kinnock replaces Michael Foot as Labour leader. For the first time, Britain becomes a net importer of manufactured goods. Beirut is riven by fighting between different religious and political groups. Hundreds of US and French troops from the UN peacekeeping force are killed by suicide bombers. US Cruise missiles arrive in Britain despite protests. An IRA bomb outside Harrods in London kills five. The IRA also kidnap the racehorse Shergar and it is never seen again.

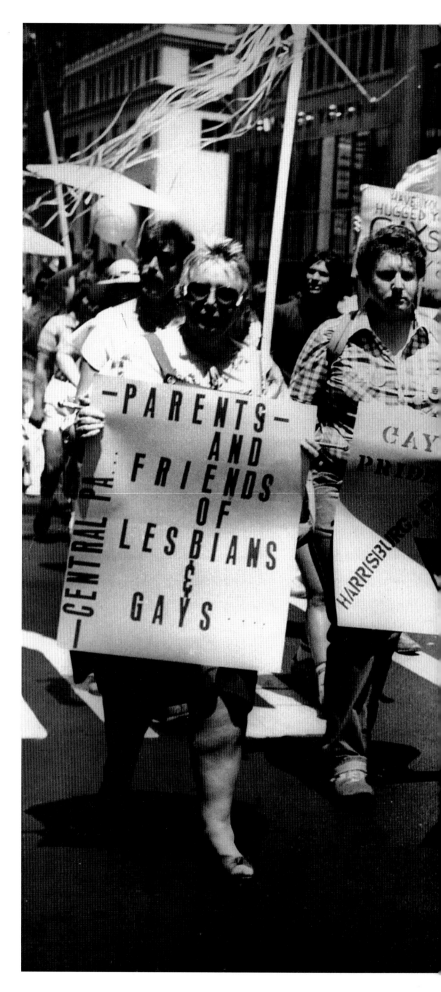

A gay rights march
in New York, with parents of lesbians and gays participating (right). *This takes place annually to commemorate the founding of the Gay Alliance after the police attack on the Stonewall Inn, a gay bar in Greenwich Village, in 1969. The figure above seems to be answering the question he holds up on his placard by implying that, with his dual sexuality, he does not have to.*

PETER KEEGAN

1984

Eight hundred thousand council houses are sold to their tenants in Britain, and British Telecom becomes the first big state-owned industry to be privatised. An IRA bomb explodes at the Conservative Party Conference in Brighton, killing four. Jerzy Popieluszko, a pro-Solidarity Catholic priest, is murdered by Polish security men. Konstantin Chernenko succeeds Andropov as Russian leader. Mrs Gandhi, the Indian Prime Minister, is killed by her Sikh bodyguards.

Famine in Ethiopia

brought on by war, drought and the outrageous half-baked Marxist regime of President Mengistu, probably kills a million this year (opposite). It is also graphically portrayed on television. The Irish rock singer Bob Geldof (above), formerly of the Boomtown Rats, makes the cause of the starving his own, raising many millions of pounds through records and concerts for his Live Aid charity.

1985

Mikhail Gorbachev becomes the new Soviet leader and has his long 'fireside chat' with President Reagan at the Geneva summit. A fire at Bradford City football ground kills fifty-two and another forty-one are killed in Brussels when Italian and Liverpudlian fans riot. Boris Becker becomes Wimbledon tennis champion, aged seventeen. CDs are replacing vinyl records and cassette tapes.

COLIN DAVEY

ALAN GLENWRIGHT

A striking miner

talks to policemen (left). Arthur Scargill (above) called out his members in March 1984 without balloting them, which immediately alienated the Nottinghamshire pits. The weather was getting warmer, there were big stockpiles of coal at the power stations, the new laws against secondary picketing had teeth, the police response was well coordinated, and long term, natural gas and oil looked well able to take the place of coal. His timing and tactics all wrong, Scargill stares defeat in the face by March this year.

1986

The 'Westland Affair' leads to the resignation of two Cabinet ministers, Leon Brittan and Michael Heseltine, in a row over financing a new helicopter. The London Stock Exchange reform, the 'Big Bang', takes place. Sacked printers fail to stop Rupert Murdoch producing the *Sun* and *The Times* at his new plant in Wapping. The world's worst nuclear accident takes place at Chernobyl power station in the Ukraine. US planes bomb Libya for supporting terrorism. A space shuttle explodes on take-off, at Cape Canaveral, killing seven astronauts. The Swedish Prime Minister, Olof Palme, is assassinated.

BRIAN HARRIS

An old lady
*who has come to take advantage of the charity
offered by the Crisis at Christmas organisation* (opposite). *The
numbers of homeless down-and-outs living on the streets of big cities,
like these young people given a roof over their heads in St James's
Church, Piccadilly* (above), *is a cause for concern. Some point the
finger at an uncaring ethos abroad in Thatcher's Britain; others
give more weight to the fragmentation of the family
under a multitude of pressures.*

1987

Stock markets round the world collapse on 'Black Monday', 19 October. A fire in King's Cross underground station kills thirty. The 'Great Storm' sweeps southern England. West German Matthias Rust lands his small plane in Moscow's Red Square undetected, giving President Gorbachev the excuse to replace his defence minister with someone willing to back his drive for detente. The USA's 'Irangate' hearings reveal how profits from the sale of arms to Iran are being used to support right-wing Contra rebels in Nicaragua. Reagan and Gorbachev sign the INF Treaty to cut nuclear arms stockpiles.

BRIAN HARRIS

The *Herald of Free Enterprise*
lies on a sandbank just outside Zeebrugge harbour in Belgium (above). Failure to shut the loading doors of this roll-on roll-off ferry results in 184 deaths. Given the ship's name, we can see in this a portentous warning about the economic reversal about to hit Britain.

The Conservatives' landslide
victory in the General Election this year sees them win many unlikely seats, but not even the irrepressible Lady Olga Maitland can take the East End stronghold of Bethnal Green and Stepney away from Labour (right).

JOHN VOOS

1988

Fire on the Piper Alpha oil rig in the North Sea kills 166. An earthquake in Armenia kills 10,000. The country is also fighting neighbouring Azerbaijan. A US warship shoots down an Iranian airliner by mistake and kills 290. George Bush is elected US President. The Palestinians' Intifada uprising against Israel begins. Pakistan's dictator Zia ul-Haq is killed in a plane crash, allowing Benazir Bhutto to be elected Prime Minister.

PETER MacDIARMID

Air and rail disasters,

ten days apart. A crash between two rush-hour commuter trains at Clapham Junction in December kills thirty-six people (above). Then a terrorist bomb brings down an American jumbo jet over the Scottish border, killing 270. A victim's foot protrudes from a smashed roof at Lockerbie, where more than forty homes are hit by falling debris (right).

DAVID ROSE

1989

The Hillsborough Stadium disaster in Sheffield results in the death of ninety-five football fans. After nine years' fighting, the last Soviet troops leave Afghanistan. A largely student occupation of Tiananmen Square in Beijing ends in violence when Deng Xiaoping sends in the tanks. Decaying at its heart, the 'Evil Empire' of Soviet-enforced Communist rule in Europe ends peaceably, except in Romania, where President Ceausescu's regime goes down and he and his wife die violently. The new drug Ecstasy powers the 'Chemical Generations' night-long acid-house dancing.

BRIAN HARRIS

East German refugees,
safely through the crumbling Iron Curtain, hug each other on Austrian soil (left). Hungary has opened its borders and so provides a roundabout route for East Germans to get out to West Germany, via itself and Austria. The Berlin Wall comes down, making this detour unnecessary, and then in December the Czechoslovaks also get rid of their Communists, and celebrate in Prague's Wenceslaus Square (above).

BRIAN HARRIS

DAVID ASHDOWN

1990

Margaret Thatcher's leadership of the Conservatives is challenged and she is replaced by John Major. The trial of those involved in illegal support of the Guinness Company's share price during its takeover of the Distillers Group in 1986 sends shock waves through the British financial world. West and East Germany are reunited. Lech Walesa is elected President of Poland. Saddam Hussein, dictator of Iraq, invades Kuwait. A massive build-up of US and other forces begins in Saudi Arabia.

Gang members
in Los Angeles (above) *are made to stand with their hands on a car bonnet (or hood) lit up by another's headlights while police frisk them for weapons. In a city where 70,000 dealers are selling crack cocaine and other drugs, heavily armed hoodlums often have more firepower than the cops, so this is a very necessary precaution.*

South African police
fire pump-action shotguns at demonstrators on the day of Nelson Mandela's release after twenty-seven years in prison (left). *His African National Congress will soon begin negotiations with President F. W. de Klerk.*

JON JONES

1991

Saddam Hussein ignores the United Nations deadline for withdrawal from Kuwait and Operation 'Desert Storm' begins on 16 January, ending on 28 February with total Iraqi defeat. Saddam then subdues rebelling Kurds in the north and Shias in the south of his country. Slovenia and Croatia break away from Yugoslavia. Serbs are soon fighting Croats. Hardline Russian Communists stage a coup against Gorbachev, but Boris Yeltsin rallies the forces of reform. The former republics within the USSR declare their independence and the Communist Party is disbanded.

BRIAN HARRIS

JOHN VOOS

BRIAN HARRIS

Burning oil wells,
*deliberately set on fire in Kuwait by the retreating Iraqis,
blot out the desert sun with a pall of smoke* (left and top).
*Saddam Hussein has also ordered oil to be pumped into the Gulf
to prevent an amphibious landing. The environmental damage
and the human misery brought about by his regime – evident
on these faces at a feeding station for those caught in
no man's land* (above) *– is incalculable.*

1992

The Conservatives win their fourth General Election in a row and John Smith replaces Neil Kinnock as Labour leader. Britain is forced to devalue its currency and leave the European Exchange Rate Mechanism. The Queen endures her *annus horribilis* with the Duke of York, the Princess Royal and the Prince of Wales divorcing or separating, and a devastating fire at Windsor Castle. Bill Clinton beats George Bush in the US Presidential election. Bosnia-Herzegovina declares independence and Serbs begin 'ethnic cleansing' there while besieging the capital of Sarajevo.

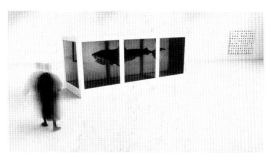

NICK TURPIN

BRIAN HARRIS

Visitors at the Tate Gallery

warily circle Anish Kapoor's Untitled *(right), working out why he won last year's Turner Prize. Showman and restaurateur Damien Hirst's shark in formaldehyde (top) is one of a number of pickled animals and parts he will have signed by the time he wins the prize in 1995. As he says, 'It's amazing what you can do with an E in A-level art, a twisted imagination and a chainsaw.' The flags and flyers for the Clinton/Gore Democratic Presidential campaign (above) hark back to the good old days of Pop Art.*

NICK TURPIN

THIS SEQUENCE TOM PILSTON

1993

Britain ratifies the Maastricht Treaty which greatly accelerates the centralising tendency of the EC, now the European Union. Pro- and anti-reform groups struggle for control of Russia, culminating in Yeltsin ordering tanks to bombard the White House parliament building. The siege of the Branch Davidian sect at Waco in Texas is badly mishandled, resulting in seventy-two deaths. Israel and Palestine sign a peace agreement in Washington. Czechoslovakia splits into the Czech and Slovak Republics. Mobile phones become hugely popular and the Internet is up and running.

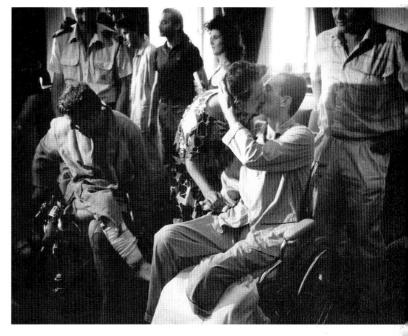

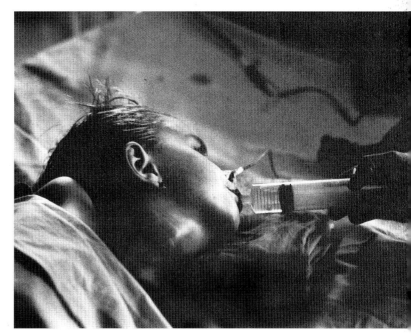

Fear in Sarajevo.

People queuing for water look up apprehensively at the sound of a sniper's shot (opposite). With plastic water containers tied to his bicycle a Sarajevan pedals hard across open ground (top left). A policeman who has lost an arm and a leg in a grenade attack kisses his bride after his marriage in hospital (top right). Five-year-old Irma, paralysed from the neck down by a fragment of a mortar bomb, is fed by syringe shortly before she is transferred to London's Great Ormond Street Hospital after the intervention of John Major (above right). A man weak from hunger is helped by passers-by (above left).

1994

The Channel Tunnel is opened. The death of John Smith gives Tony Blair the leadership of the Labour Party. The IRA announce a ceasefire in Northern Ireland. Up to half a million, mostly Tutsi, Rwandans are massacred and 1½ million become refugees. The first multi-racial elections are held in South Africa and Nelson Mandela becomes President. Britain's first National Lottery draw is held. Steven Spielberg wins an Oscar for *Schindler's List*.

DAVID ROSE

TOM PILSTON

An American D-Day veteran
closes his eyes and perhaps remembers his dead comrades who never made it off Omaha Beach in Normandy on 6 June, fifty years ago.

British veterans
ring their wives from Portsmouth before setting out across the Channel for the commemorations in Normandy.

1995

An employee of Barings bank loses £620 million in the Singapore futures market, which leads to the collapse of the bank. A peace treaty is signed by the warring factions in Bosnia. Russian forces do badly against Chechen nationalists in the Caucasus. America is shocked by the right-wing extremist bombing of a Federal building in Oklahoma. Among the many victims are children aged between one and seven. Israeli Prime Minister Yitzhak Rabin is assassinated by a Jewish extremist. An earthquake in Kobe, Japan, kills 5,000 and destroys over 100,000 buildings. *Pulp Fiction* and *Four Weddings and a Funeral* are the popular films.

TOM PILSTON

A ceasefire maybe,
*but the Army still has a presence on the
Falls Road in Belfast, with a mural of the Virgin
and Child as a backdrop.*

No flash cars
*with which to pull the girls in Cuba,
in fact very few cars at all in this embattled Socialist
dictatorship, deserted by its erstwhile Soviet
allies and under economic blockade
from the USA.*

TOM PILSTON

BRIAN HARRIS

1996

A government warning is given about BSE, the 'mad cow disease', spreading to humans, sparking a crisis in the British beef industry. The IRA cease-fire ends with bombs in London's Docklands and Manchester city centre. The Chechnya–Russia war ends in victory for the Chechens. Taliban fundamentalists control much of Afghanistan including Kabul. Bill Clinton is re-elected as US President and Benjamin Netanyahu takes control in Israel with his hawkish Likud Party.

Sixteen children and a teacher

are killed by a crazed gunman at Dunblane Primary School in Scotland. He then kills himself. Flowers and wreaths are left by mourners trying to express their grief and assuage their shock. In response to public pressure, the Government later bans all handguns.

1997

Tony Blair becomes Prime Minister with a Labour majority of 179 seats in the British General Election. In the Devolution referendums Scotland and Wales vote for separate assemblies. William Hague succeeds John Major as Conservative leader. The IRA ceasefire is renewed and its representatives enter peace talks. Princess Diana is killed in a car crash in Paris. Hong Kong is handed back to the Chinese. Laurent Kabila ousts General Mobutu from Zaire. Deng Xiaoping dies, aged ninety-two, and Jiang Zemin becomes the leading figure in China.

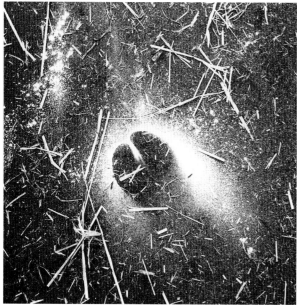

BRIAN HARRIS

The ghostly hoofprint

of a cow or bullock stands for the many
thousands of beasts being slaughtered in a
desperate gesture to try and dispel the fears
aroused by the BSE beef scare.

A hunt saboteur

raises his stick and a huntsman
his whip in a confrontation. In July a
pro-hunting rally in Hyde Park attracts 100,000
mostly country people, many who have never
followed hounds on horseback, but all
passionately opposed to the threat to their
way of life which they see in the new
private member's bill to ban the sport.
In 1998 300,000 will march through
London for the same cause,
and the bill will fail.

TOM PILSTON

1998

A Northern Ireland peace agreement is brokered and then endorsed by a referendum there and in the Republic. President Clinton continues to be dogged by accusations of sexual scandal, with Monica Lewinsky replacing Paula Jones as the biggest threat to his reputation. The 'Tiger Economies' of South-East Asia fall one after another into recession and this brings an end to the long dictatorship of President Suharto of Indonesia. The Nigerian dictator General Abacha dies. India and then Pakistan carry out nuclear weapons tests. In Kosovo in former Yugoslavia there is fighting between the Albanian majority and the Serbs. Weather patterns around the globe are disturbed by the activities of the Pacific current El Niño, increasing fears of global warming.

A Lapland forest,
and the encroachment of man upon it,
is turned into a warning of what can be lost by the
Finnish photographer Jorma Puranen. 'A closed museum'
is the translation of the elegantly lettered Latin in the
foreground, reminding us of the animal and plant
species that may disappear, or never be discovered,
because of the destruction of their habitat.

JORMA PURANEN

1999

The Millennium Dome is taking shape at Greenwich, an exhibition marking the end of this century, just as one marked its beginning. Now, in an age of theme parks and interactive displays, when we are constantly being bombarded with sophisticated imagery, we must wait and see whether 'The Millennium Experience' will prove that we have outgrown shows such as this. But with £750 million spent and New Labour firmly committed to it, failure won't come from lack of funds or political will.

Richard Rogers Partnership Dome,
when complete, will be the largest cable net-supported structure in the world, and is at present the biggest single construction project in Europe. By adopting a teflon-coated fibreglass covering its life will be extended from twelve to twenty-five years. Its interior space
 *amounts to thirteen Albert Halls or two Wembley Stadiums.*

BRIAN HARRIS

How to buy or license a picture from this book

Picture Licensing Information

To license the pictures listed below please call

Getty Images + 44 171 266 2662 or email info@getty-images.com your picture selection with the page/reference numbers

Hulton Getty Online

All of the pictures listed below and countless others are available via Hulton Getty Online at:
http://www.hultongetty.com

Buying a print

For details of how to purchase exhibition quality prints call
The Hulton Getty Picture Gallery
+ 44 171 376 4525

The Hulton Getty Picture Collection, originally formed in 1947 as the Hulton Press Library, contains over 12 million images, some of which date from the earliest days of photography. It includes original material from leading press agencies – Topical Press, Keystone, Central Press, Fox Photos and the General Photographic Agency as well as from *Picture Post*, the *Daily Express* and the *Evening Standard*. Page/reference numbers as styled below.

To purchase copies of photographs from the *Independent* for reproduction or commercial use please contact
Picture Syndication, the *Independent*, telephone + 44 171 293 2777, fax + 44 171 293 2488, stating subject of photograph, photographer's name, page reference and intended use. These photographs are also available for personal use (some restrictions may apply), size 12"x 9". Please contact **Independent Photographs, telephone + 44 171 293 2534, fax + 44 171 293 2488.**

Picture acknowledgements

Alan Band 137, 157; Steve Benbow 159; Gamma Liaison: Walker Evans 81, Charles Nye 153, Raphael Wollman 173; Ernst Haas Studios 101; Peter Keegan 175; V Kinelovsky/Slava Katamidze Collection 94; The *Observer*: Allan Glenwright 179, Don McCullin 139, David Newell Smith 155

Pictures from the *Independent*

David Ashdown 189; Brian Harris front and back cover, 6, 180–182, 186–187, 190–192, 200, 202, 207; Peter Jay 4; Jon Jones 188; Herbie Knott half-title; Peter Macdiarmid 184; Tom Pilston 194–195, 197–199, 203; David Rose 185, 196; Nick Turpin 192–193; John Voos 183, 191.

Pictures from Photo 98

Stanley Greene/Vu 5
Jorma Puranen 205